MARTIN LUTHER KING JR.

His Religion, His Philosophy

THE ROLE OF THE CHURCH IN SOCIAL JUSTICE

RT. HON. REV. DR. PHILIP A. RAHMING

Genre
Library Solutions

Martin Luther King Jr.: His Religion, His Philosophy by
Rt. Hon. Rev. Dr. Philip A. Rahming

Copyright © 2024 by **Rt. Hon. Rev. Dr. Philip A. Rahming**

E-book: 979-8-3303-5420-7
Paperback: 979-8-3303-5419-1
Hardback: 979-8-3303-5421-4

Printed in the United States of America.

Genre Library Solutions
300 Delaware Ave. Suite 210,
Wilmington, DE 19801
www.genrelibrarysolutions.com
(315) 367-7314

This book is dedicated to my parents Lennie Arthur and Rebecca Rahming deceased, to my twin sisters Lenora deceased and Isadora, my four nieces, Cheryl deceased, Jewel Ann, Windy and Kesna

Books by Rev. Dr. Philip A. Rahming, J.P.

- *MARTIN LUTHER KING, JR.: His Religion, His Philosophy*

- *A New Beginning*

- *The Unsigned, Undelivered Letter: Pindling Left Free… Mandela Set Free*

CONTENTS

ACKNOWLEDGEMENTS

I am indebted to Dr. Henlee H. Barnette, former Professor of Christian Ethics at Southern Baptist Theological Seminary, Louisville, Kentucky. He guided me and supervised this research into Martin Luther King's ecclesiology. Dr. Frederick G. Sampson II, former pastor of Mt. Lebanon Baptist Church, Louisville, Kentucky and former pastor of Tabernacle Missionary Baptist Church, Detroit, Michigan, personally inspired me to write the book. In Detroit in 1974, Dr. Sampson introduced me to Rosa Parks, whose tired feet triggered the Montgomery Bus Boycott which eventually led to the Civil Rights Movement led by Dr. Martin Luther King, Jr. I must record also the encouragements I received from Dr. C. B. Lucas, former pastor of Emmanuel Baptist Church, Louisville, Kentucky.

For typing my manuscript, I am very grateful to Mrs. Marion Debbie Goodman-Ferguson, of the Student Services of the College of The Bahamas, and to Miss Julieth Roslyn Lightbourn, of the Personnel Department of the College. Rosemary Munroe, a business student at the college, and Norma Edgecombe, Dean B.A., a Ministry of Education Teacher at Palmdale Primary School, assisted me in my proofreading. My thanks go to Wendy Shenna Rahming, Cartwright B.A. in Commercial Arts at the American College, Atlanta, Georgia, for suggesting the cover design.

FOREWORD

In January, 1986, for the first time, the people of the United States of America officially recognized the historical importance of the life and work of Civil Rights leader, Martin Luther King, Jr. by observing his birthday as a national public holiday. The debate surrounding the establishment of this holiday focused renewed attention upon King the man, the minister, and the leader as well as on the cause for which he so ardently struggled and for which he eventually died.

This present volume is, therefore, a timely addition to that body of literature which explores the nature of the greatness of Martin Luther King and his work. A Baptist minister himself, the author, Philip Rahming, emphasizes particularly the significance of the black church in the United States as the vehicle through which King's non-violent philosophy was able to find expression and be put into meaningful action. Their churches were the institutions which blacks genuinely controlled for themselves, and it was from their churches that they had traditionally drawn strength and hope in their many struggles. Dr. Rahming demonstrates also how King's family heritage, his education, his theological and philosophical training and, especially, his own concept of the church and its purpose in the world all combined to prepare him for the very special role he was to play in the lives of his people.

In a relatively few pages, then, Dr. Rahming highlights many of the important threads which, when woven together, made up the fabric of the life, thought, beliefs and actions of Martin Luther King. He is to be commended for undertaking this worthwhile and useful work.

Keva M. Bethel, Ph.D.
Principal
College of The Bahamas

PREFACE

Martin Luther King, Jr., was well aware of the pervasiveness and ideological character of evil in his time. He came to believe that the way of reconciliation and nonviolence was the only ideal way to deal with evil and to affect social change.[1] He did not accept the evil structure generated by modern relativism, viz., ideological conflict. Rather he opposed relativism with the Christian faith. In King's theology God was supreme. Faith in Him affirms reconciliation. Relativism denied such possibility.[2] It is the nature and function of the church to oppose relativism with a faith and a commitment which will open it to a transcending redemptive reality.

The Civil Rights Movement seems in some respect identical with the mission and hope of the black church in America. For more than three hundred years, the church was the center of the spiritual and social life of blacks. In the church the blacks identified themselves directly with the struggles of the children of Israel down in the land of Egypt. Through the years, as progress was made to dispel their hardships and to take them nearer to the event of acceptability by the white community, the blacks saw themselves moving out and away from Egypt's bondage. The march is always toward the promised land of freedom. There, at last, they would have the privilege and the ability to shape their own destiny.

In Montgomery, Alabama, the black church stood firm behind the Bus Boycott and King, the Baptist preacher, who was its spokesman. It was at last their long hope and their loss of fear. It was what Sir Winston S. Churchill would call "their stick-to-itiveness" that gave the Civil Rights Movement the punch that staggered the nation and made the whole world aware of the black man's fight for freedom and social justice in America.

As a foreign student at Southern Baptist Theological Seminary, Louisville, Kentucky, 1969-71, I was greatly impressed by the position Martin Luther King Jr., the Baptist pastor-preacher, took in the Civil Rights Movement to bring dignity to the American blacks. In 1965, the year of my graduation at Calabar Theological College, Kingston, Jamaica, I heard Dr. King speak at the University of the West Indies. In the fall of 1968, I met and talked with Dr. King's parents in Atlanta, Georgia. Then later in that same year, I had talks with A.D. Williams King, brother to Martin. In 1974, I met and spoke with Rosa Parks in Detroit. From these conversations, I became more deeply interested in the prophetic ministry of Martin Luther King Jr., especially his view of the church and its role in the Civil Rights Movement.

I wanted to discover a concept of the church as understood and practiced by Martin Luther King during his involvement in the Civil Rights Movement from the Montgomery Bus Boycott in 1955 to his death in Memphis on April 4, 1968. This book is a focus upon his concept of the church and its role in social justice.

EPIGRAPH

God Bless Our Sunny Clime [1]*

God bless our sunny clime, spur us to heights sublime
To keep men free. Let brothers, sisters stand
Firm, trusting, hand in hand thro'out Bahama land
One brotherhood, one brotherhood.

Let gratefulness ascend, courageous deeds extend
From isle to isle. Long let us treasure peace
So may our lives increase, our prayers never cease
Let freedom ring!
Let freedom ring!

The long, long night has passed, the morning breaks at last
From shore to shore. Sunrise with golden gleam,
Sons, daughters, share a dream, for one working team
One brotherhood, one brotherhood.

Not for this time nor for this chosen few alone
We pledge ourselves. Live loyal to our God,
Love country, friend and foe, Oh help us by thy might,
Great God our King! Great God our King!

1

The Gathering Storms

This chapter presents the man, Martin Luther King, Jr., and describes the factors which contributed to the role he assumed in the Civil Right Movement. This chapter also sets the scenes which Led to his entry into the struggle for racial justice. It also discusses King's inner struggle against the church and then his preparation for the church as pastor and as the agent for moral and social change.

Adam Daniel Williams, Martin's maternal grandfather, was born in the year of Lincoln's Emancipation Proclamation. He was a hard-going, deliberate man. He took a course in theology at Morehouse College in Atlanta, but Williams clung to the faith of his forefathers. His *learning* did not interfere with his *burning*.

A. D. Williams became a Baptist preacher and therefore a leader in the very first of the black community's free institutions the church. The Reverend Mr. Williams pastored Ebenezer Baptist Church in Atlanta where many black people gathered for worship. It was the church where the blacks received spiritual power as well as physical and mental release. The church was their social center. It was the place where they got their important information about God and about their world.

Adam D. Williams practically built Ebenezer Baptist Church. For a while, he was president of the local National Association for the Advancement of Colored People. He was a powerful member of the Negro Citizens group that established Booker T. Washington High School and a YMCA branch to Atlanta's Negro community. Williams was in the forefront in organizing the boycott by black readers which finally killed the daily *Georgian*. In 1931, the veteran pastor-preacher died, and Martin Luther King, Sr., his son-in- law, succeeded him at Ebenezer.

Martin Luther King, Sr. soon became a leader of those blacks who resented and opposed the indignities of segregation in Atlanta, Georgia. Like his father-in-law, he too was a power in the local NAACP branch. King, Sr. was a force to be reckoned with in Atlanta's Negro Voters' League. He refused to use the services of Atlanta's segregated buses. King fought to obtain equal pay for black teachers. He was successful in integrating the courthouse elevators.

Martin Luther King, Sr. met stern opposition. He received threatening letters from the Ku Klux Klan, and he received threats and insults over the telephone. But he did not give up the struggle. He made up his mind to oppose the system unto his death. King, Sr. said he would never accept the system no matter how long it lasted.[3] This was his resolution.

At the age of twenty-six, King, Sr. received a high school diploma. By that time, he was serving as pastor of two small Baptist churches. He enrolled as a student at Morehouse College. In her book, Coretta said even with his church and family responsibilities, her father-in-law continued his studies.[4] He possessed a stubborn courage and determination to go on when most men would drop out. But hard work brought its rewards. He became prominent both in the civic and religious affairs of his people. The Reverend Mr. King became a trustee of Atlanta University, Morris Brown College, and Morehouse College.

On Thanksgiving Day, 1926, Martin Luther King, Sr. married Albertha, the daughter of Reverend A.D. Williams. Three years later, Martin Luther King, Jr. was born at noon on a chilly Tuesday, January 15, 1929, in Atlanta, Georgia.

The son of a Baptist minister, he enjoyed a comfortable childhood. The Auburn Avenue black bourgeoisie were hardly affected by the plague of unemployment brought on by the Depression. But despite the relative comfort and security, this baby was black. He was born into a system which placed blacks automatically in an inferior position to white people.

The classification in America went back as far as three hundred years. Despite these conditions, in twenty-eight years the babe became the youngest person to win the NAACP's Springarn Medal, awarded each year to the person making the greatest contribution in race relations. At thirty- five, Martin Luther King was named "Man of the Year" by *Time* on January 3, 1964. Later the same year, Thursday, December 10, he became the third black, the second black American, the twelfth American, and the youngest ever to receive the Nobel Peace Prize. And now, beginning in 1986 and 18 years after his death, Americans celebrates his birthday on the third Monday in January every year. King becomes the first Negro and the second American whose birthday is celebrated as a national holiday. President George Washington, America's first president, is the first.

"I Want to be like Jesus." This was King's favorite song as a child. At the age of four, he took a deep breath and sang it with gusto before the delegates of a Baptist Convention. As he sang, a few people would break in and shout, "Amen." As a child, he had a flare for big words- words which moved people. He watched his father do that every Sunday morning. He said to his mother that someday he himself would get some big words and that she should just wait and see.[5] In the home, King, along with his sister and brother, were taught that education was the key to a useful life and that the church was the key to moral life.

During his youth, Martin lived in a spacious twelve-room frame house on Auburn Avenue at the foot of Atlanta's famous Peachtree Street. There was always meat on the table and Sunday clothes, plus allowances and bicycles for the children. However, he encountered several incidents which, at his early age, made him aware that he was black and that being black was regarded as inferior by the white man. When he was six, the mother of two of his white playmates told him that her boys were becoming too old to play with "niggers." At eight, he witnessed his father's unsuccessful attempt to purchase a pair of shoes in the front section of a downtown store. On another occasion, a policeman stopped his father's car for failing to observe a stop sign. The officer addressed the old man as "boy." But the Baptist preacher said that he was the Reverend King. He pointed to his son as the boy. Then he told his son to tell the officer his name.[6]

One day his mother took King to a downtown store and told him to wait there until she returned. He was eleven at the time. While he stood waiting for his mother, a white woman, a stranger, came to him and accused him of being "the little nigger who stepped on her foot." Then she struck him with a stunning blow on his cheek. The boy's only response was to stand where his mother left him.

King came close to hating white people when a bus driver ordered him and some other black students to give up their seats for white passengers. They were returning from a speech contest. At first they refused, but later they consented and had to stand on their feet for ninety minutes on a trip back to Atlanta.

Besides arriving at the near point of hating the white man, such inconsiderate treatment could make one feel and become worthless. But King's parents taught him that a life is worth something when it is moral. He never forgot his mother's advice when his two white friends became too old to play with blacks. She assured him that he was as good as anyone and warned him not to forget it.[7]

His involvement later at Morehouse in the Intercollegiate Council revealed to him that all whites were not enemies of blacks. Profoundly impressed, he recalled later the genuine relationship he experienced in the Council. It convinced King that the blacks had white allies, especially of the younger generation. Though he had gotten to the point of resenting all whites, his frequent association with them, softened his resentment. King found the spirit of cooperation overcoming resentment in his heart.[8]

When King was five, he demanded that he go to school with his older sister. He was enrolled in his sister's School, on the first grade. On describing his recent fifth birthday party to his class, the secret got out and out went King. Shortly he turned six and was legally enrolled in the first grade.

After completing grade school, King attended Laboratory High School. This school was progressive with a national rating. He was a B-plus student. After two years, he was transferred to Booker T. Washington High in Atlanta. At fifteen, he was ready for college.

Martin Luther King enrolled at Morehouse College in September, 1944, one of the 206 fresh men that year. Morehouse was the school attended by both Adam D. Williams, his maternal grandfather, and Martin, Sr., his father. Both men entered the Baptist ministry and played important roles in civic and religious spheres. In spite of his deep roots in the black Baptist Church and ministry, King decided against the ministry as early as during his high school days. He felt that the church had become irrelevant and that by becoming a physician he would make a better contribution to his people.

King disliked the hand clapping and shouting characteristics of the black church. For him, the church was too emotional and not rational enough. He felt religion should be more intellectual and thoughtful. The church, he believed, should take an interest in the life of man on earth as well as in heaven. He felt that the church should concern itself with the problems of racism, unemployment, poverty, and education. His entire first two years at Morehouse were spent in thinking, reading, searching, discussing and asking questions about these issues.

King excelled in oratory. He was the recipient of an Elks Club award for a speech called "The Negro and the Constitution." At Morehouse College, he took second place in the Webb Oratorical Contest while still in his sophomore year. King signed up as a sociology major and buckled down to his studies. Here, for the first time, he participated in an open discussion on racial injustice. There in his class he heard for the first time that segregation was morally wrong and that it must be abolished. His sociology teacher, Professor Walter Chivers, told the class again and again that money as well as race was the root of evil.[9]

Martin Luther King, entered Morehouse with the intention of going on to law. Earlier, he felt the urge to do medicine. But now each day he was being attracted to the ministry. Finally, in Kings junior year, he decided to study for the ministry. King wrote an article entitled, "The Purpose of Education" which was printed in the Maroon Tiger, the college student paper. In it he said that education should equip a person to think scientifically and logically. It should enable him to distinguish the true from the false, facts from fiction. Hence, he concluded that a logical person would learn to reject the theory of racial superiority.

In 1947, at the age of seventeen, King preached his trial sermon and was later ordained. In his eighteenth year, he became the assistant minister to his father at Ebenezer Baptist Church in Atlanta, Georgia. The following year, he graduated from Morehouse College with a Bachelor of Arts Degree. King won a scholarship to Crozer Theological Seminary in Chester, Pennsylvania. He was present in September, 1948, to begin the next three years of his theological studies. He made a better academic record at Crozer than at Morehouse, graduating as valedictorian of his class.

In addition to his regular class work at Crozer, King took courses in philosophy at the University of Pennsylvania. He was searching for new ideas that would wipe out racial injustice. At Crozer, King became acquainted with the social gospel. What left an indelible imprint on his mind was Rauschenbusch's insistence that the gospel deals with the whole man, not only his soul but his body; not only his spiritual well-being but his material well-being. Rauschenbusch convinced King that any religion which was only concerned with the souls of men and disregards their social and economic conditions was a dead and useless religion.[10]

King also read the works of Reinhold Niebuhr. The realistic and prophetic elements put in the passionate style of Niebuhr coupled with his profound thought appealed to King. He became so taken by Niebuhr's social ethics that he almost made Niebuhr's conclusion his.[11]

For example, King said that true pacifism is not unrealistic submission to evil power, as Niebuhr contends. It is a courageous confrontation of evil by the power of love in the belief that it is better to be the receiver of violence than the doer of it. Violence multiplies the existence of violence and bitterness in the world. The power of love develops a sense of shame in the enemy and brings about a transformation and change of heart.

Niebuhr reminded him, however, that human motives are complex. King concluded that Niebuhr's stress on man's sinfulness was excessive and that his rejection of pacifism in the name of realism was unwarranted.

While King was at Boston University, he came to understand that Niebuhr overemphasized corruption. He concluded that Reinhold Niebuhr was so involved in the diagnosis of man's sin sickness that he paid no attention to his cure by the grace of God[12]

While a student at Morehouse, King read Henry David Thoreau's essay on "Civil Disobedience." Thoreau argued that no man should obey a law which he feels is unjust. Instead, he should be willing to take the punishment set by society for breaking such law. The best place for a good man is jail when the society makes unjust laws.

Karl Marx, also interested King. He believed that Marx's dictatorial methods for eliminating injustice denied the dignity of man. They were not Christian as indeed the laws of segregation were. But at the same time, King saw that Communism challenged every Christian to a growing concern about social justice. The writings of Marx revealed the danger of the profit motive as the only basis of an economic system. Capitalism tends to inspire men only to make a living but never to make a life. The success of living is judged by the index of a man's salary or by the size of his car. The quality of his service or his relationship to humanity is hardly ever considered. Thoreau's non violent resistance method seemed better to King. But at the same time, he continued his search through the writings of great minds. His aim was to discover a way to use the principles of love and brotherhood as a force against injustice. An acceptable theory was the key.

In his search for a viable methodology, King passed through a season of doubt. Nietzsche's philosophy disturbed his faith in love. His hope in the power of love to solve social problems began to die.[13] King read parts of *The Genealogy of Morals* and all of *The Will to Power*. Nietzsche glorified power. It was a result of his contempt for ordinary morals. He attacked the roots of Hebraic Christian morality, despising virtues like piety and humility. He could not bear the glorification of meekness, which he called weakness. Nietzsche looked for a developed superman who would surpass man as man surpassed the ape.

Dr. Mordecai Johnson, president of Howard University in Washington, D.C., tried without success to conquer racial injustice by preaching sermons on brotherly love. He told a congregation one Sunday morning about the Indian named Mahatma Gandhi. Through the power of love and without approving the firing of one shot or uttering a violent word, he led his people from the British rule. In the audience that Sunday morning was an excited Martin Luther King. For the next few weeks, he read all he could find about this Gandhi. The search soon came to an end. A theory was found. The key was available, for he was convinced that love could do it.

Gandhi's concept of "Satyagraha" was profoundly significant to King. "Satya" is truth, the equivalent of love. "Agraha" is force. Satyagraha means, therefore, truth-force or love-force. Before King read Mahatma Gandhi he was almost convinced that the ethics of Jesus was only applicable in individual relationships. They did not apply when, for example, racial groups and nations were in conflict. Then, a more realistic method seemed necessary. His understanding of Gandhi revealed to him the efficacy of the ethics of Jesus in all human relationships.[14] King had discovered that Gandhi read Thoreau's "Civil Disobedience."

All Martin Luther King needed was a door to try the key. He kept that key in his pocket; he retained that combination in his heart and mind until a door was found. It was not until Thursday, December 1, 1955, in Montgomery, Alabama, that a door began to indicate itself. And King was there with his key.

Three years of studies quickly came to an end, and Martin Luther King received his Bachelor of Divinity Degree from Crozer. He was voted the student most likely to succeed. He received the school's highest award for scholarship, and was awarded the Lewis Crozer Fellowship for two years of graduate study in any college. He chose Boston University.

King began work on his Doctor of Philosophy Degree in September, 1951. After spending a few months in Boston, Martin met Coretta Scott. Miss Scott was a graduate student at New England Conservatory of Music. She was born in Heiberger, Alabama. At the time Martin met her, she was a soprano preparing herself for a career as a concert singer. Martin and Coretta were married on June 18, 1953. Following their marriage in Perry County, Alabama, the couple returned to Boston to resume studies. The next June Mrs. King graduated from the conservatory, and in the summer of that same year, King completed all work toward earning his degree except for his thesis.

In his thesis, King attempted to resolve the controversy between Dr. Paul Tillich, a German, and Dr. Henry Wieman, an American, who disagreed over the nature of God. It was the task of Martin

Luther King to summarize the writings of both men and to attempt to clarify the controversy. His investigation led him to the conclusion that Tillich believed God was Power and Being. Wieman believed God was Goodness and Value.

King continued his intellectual pilgrimage to nonviolence at Boston University. At Boston University he had the opportunity to talk and discuss with many exponents of non-violence. They were among the student body and visitors to the campus.[15]

Dean Walter Muelder and Professor Allen Knight Chambers had a deep sympathy for pacifism. Both men had a passion for social justice that came from a deep faith in the possibilities of human beings when they let themselves become co-workers with God. Under the stimulation and guidance of Edgar S. Brightman and L. Harold DeWolf, King studied personalistic philosophy, the theory that the clue to the meaning of ultimate reality is found in personality. Personal idealism remained King's basic philosophical position. Personalism insists that only personality, finite or infinite is ultimately real. This stimulated King into meaningful directions. First, it gave him a metaphysical and philosophical grounding for the idea of a personal God, and second, it provided him with a metaphysical basis for the dignity and worth of all human personality.

King disagreed with Hegel's absolute idealism because it tended to swallow up the many in the all-embracing one. But Hegel's contention that "truth is the whole" moved King to a philosophical method of rational coherence. Hegel's analysis of the dialectical process enabled him to understand that growth is achieved through struggle.

During 1954, one church in Massachusetts and one in New York expressed interest in calling the Reverend Martin Luther King. Three colleges offered him attractive and challenging opportunities - one a teaching post, one a deanship and the other an administrative position. In the meantime, the Dexter Avenue Baptist Church in Montgomery, Alabama, had its eyes on King. It was a comparatively small church. The membership was in the neighborhood of three hundred, but it occupied a central place in the community.

Many influential and respected citizens made up the church roll. Some were professional folks with substantial incomes. The church, moreover, had a long tradition of an educated ministry. King visited them and preached, his topic "The Three Dimensions of a Complete Life."

One month after he preached the sermon, the church extended him a call to be pastor. It was not an easy decision for Martin Luther King to make. On the one hand, he was inclined toward the pastorate; on the other, toward educational work. The Kings made the call a matter of prayer. After discussing the pros and cons, they came to a decision. They decided that in spite of the disadvantages and personal sacrifices to them, their greatest service could be done in their native South. And they felt it a moral responsibility to return to the South if only for the first few years of their ministry.

On September 1, 1954, King and his wife, Coretta, moved into the parsonage on South Jackson Street. While Mrs. King spent time converting the parsonage into a home and getting to know the ladies of the church, the pastor familiarized himself with church routine. He preached his first sermon as pastor in May of 1954.

Dexter Avenue Baptist Church was known as the "big folks" church. It catered to the upper-class blacks. Worship and traditional religious education were the chief activities of the church. The Training Union developed lay leadership but channeled it directly into the congregation in teaching Bible classes. The Missionary Society also followed the traditional pattern of reaching an elite class for the church without relating it to the changing community.

The new minister was concerned with broadening the auxiliary program of the church to include everybody. So he added the following committees:

1. a committee to revitalize Religious Education
2. a Social Service Committee
3. a Social and Political Committee
4. a committee to raise funds and administer scholarship funds for high-school graduates
5. a Cultural Committee to give encouragement to promising artists.

The congregation heartily approved these committees, and almost immediately, the membership began to grow.

After Martin Luther King got the new programs of the church on their way, he joined the local branch of the NAACP and took an active part in the life and work of the community. Through this organization, he came face to face with some of the racial problems that plagued the community. He found that most of the energies and the funds of the local NAACP were being used to defend Jeremiah Reeves. Reeves, a drummer in a black band, was arrested at the age of sixteen and accused of raping a white woman. Finally on March 28, 1958, he was electrocuted for a crime he denied committing.

The young pastor of Dexter Avenue Church joined the Alabama Council on Human Relations, an interracial group in Montgomery. This council sought to attain equal opportunity for all the people of Alabama, operating on the philosophy that all men were created equal under God. Through this organization the channels of communication were kept open between whites and blacks. The NAACP's method of integration was through legislation and court action, while the Council sought the same goal through research and action. King felt that both approaches were necessary. For through education, attitudes could be changed, and behavior could be regulated through legislation and court orders.[16]

King discovered disunity in the black community. Several civic groups existed, but each was in competition with the other. For this reason blacks could not come together for any concerted effort against the common enemy. Early in 1955, the Citizens Coordinating Committee was formed to achieve unity of thought and action. But this committee failed in its goal and was finally dissolved.

The callousness of the educated blacks also posed a problem toward unity. The majority of them never took part in efforts to better racial conditions. Some of their lack of concern was based on fear of losing their sources of economic support. Apathy among black ministers was very much in evidence. They manifested the all too common attitudes of ministers who hold that it is not the function of the church to get involved in such earthly matters as social and economic improvements. Another alarming fact was the complacent attitude of many uneducated blacks toward segregation. They, like the more educated blacks, feared economic reprisals. Hence, they avoided antagonizing the white community upon which they depended for their livelihood.

To sum up, King found division, complacency and passivity among leaders as well as the masses in the total black community. There appeared to be little hope for unity in social concern and action in the black community. Beneath the surface, however, there were the rumblings of discontent against the indignities and inequities to which blacks were being subjected.

One of the most explosive points was transportation on the city-wide buses of Montgomery. Here blacks were daily subjected to the indignities of segregation. On the buses they were sometimes called black cows and black apes. Every now and then a black would pay his bus fare at the front door and then the driver would force him to get off and reboard the bus at the rear. Before he had time to reach the rear door, the bus would pull away.

The practice of forcing the blacks to stand over empty seats in the buses was humiliating. Blacks sitting in the unreserved seats immediately behind the whites were always ordered to stand so that whites could sit. Shortly after Martin King arrived in Montgomery, Claudette Colvin was arrested for refusing to surrender her seat to a white passenger. The black community felt that the buses should be boycotted in protest. Instead a Citizens Committee was formed to meet with the management of the Bus Company and with the City Commission concerning its policy of seating on buses. King was one of those chosen to serve on the Citizens Committee.

In the meeting, the black committee was told and assured that no such incident would happen again. J. E. Bagley, Manager of the Montgomery City Lines, admitted that the driver was wrong in having Miss Colvin arrested. Police Commissioner Birmingham agreed to have the city attorney give a ruling on the policy of seating on city buses. But King lamented later that while they felt the meetings were hopeful, nothing was being done. Humiliation continued. Laws were never clarified by the city attorney. Meanwhile Claudette Colvin was convicted with a suspended sentence.[17]

As a result of the inaction of the local officials of government, long-repressed feelings of resentment on the part of blacks began to express themselves openly. Fear and apathy began to die. A new spirit of courage, self-respect and "somebodiness" began to emerge. It was during these times when the longings and aspirations of nearly 50,000 people, tired people, came to know it was more honorable to walk the streets in dignity than to ride the buses in humiliation. And it was during such times when Rosa Parks' tired feet got her arrested on the Cleveland Avenue Bus in downtown Montgomery. She was too tired to give up her seat because of those feet for anybody anymore. She was walking and standing too long.

2

From Montgomery To Memphis

In this chapter, a somewhat chronological survey of the Movement from Montgomery to Memphis will be made. The philosophy of nonviolence is discussed. However, the major emphasis here is to give a rather detailed account of the experiences of the black man and his plight during the Movement and the help he got from his church to endure.

Rosa Parks, a 42-year-old seamstress at the Montgomery Fair Department Store, was arrested in Montgomery, Alabama, on Thursday, December 1, 1955 for refusing to give up her seat on the Cleveland Avenue bus. The arrest of Mrs. Parks was the straw that broke the camel's back. In an early morning telephone call to Dr. King the day after the arrest, E.D. Nixon said they had taken that type of thing too long. He felt that the time had come to boycott the buses, for it was the only way to make white folks understand that the blacks would not take that sort of treatment any more.[18]

A protest meeting was held in the evening of December 2 at the Dexter Avenue Baptist Church. Doctors, lawyers, businessmen, government employees, union leaders, and a number of black ministers were present. The presence of ministers was particularly welcomed. To Mrs. King, it was a recognition that they were beginning to accept her husband's view that religion dealt both with heaven and earth.[19]

It was unanimously agreed to stage a Bus Boycott on Monday, December 5, 1955. This was carried out successfully. But following the conviction of Mrs. Parks on that same day, another protest meeting was held. This meeting resulted in the birth of the Montgomery

Improvement Association, and Martin Luther King, Jr. was elected president.

The birth of the Movement could not be explained without a divine dimension. Mrs. Coretta King points out that her husband sincerely believed there was a creative force at work in the world to pull down mountains of evil and level hilltops of injustice. King regarded himself as an instrument of such a force. He was convinced that God was still at work in history performing his wonders.[20]

Martin Luther King regarded the Montgomery Bus Boycott as a massive withdrawal of cooperation from an evil system. He explained that the concern was not to put the bus company out of business but to put justice into business.[21] Recalling Thoreau's words, King pointed out that whoever passively accepts evil is as much involved in it as the person who helps to perpetrate it. Anyone who accepts evil without protesting is really cooperating with it.[22]

The philosophy of nonviolence played a positive role in the Montgomery Movement. King mentioned six basic aspects of this philosophy.

First, nonviolent resistance is not a method for cowards; it does resist. While the nonviolent resister remains passive in that he is not physically aggressive toward the enemy, his mind and his emotions remain active, seeking continuously to reveal his opponent's misdeeds. Physically, the method is passive, but it is strongly active spiritually. It is active nonviolent resistance to evil.

Second, nonviolence does not seek to defeat or to humiliate the oppressor. The method is to win friendship and understanding. Noncooperation or boycotts are means of expressing protests. They are means to awaken a sense of moral shame in the opponent. The end is redemption and reconciliation, a new community of brotherliness.

Third, this method directs its attack against the evil system rather than the men who are servants of the system. The nonviolent resister seeks to defeat evil, not the individuals who are victimized by it.

Fourth, nonviolent resistance is a willingness to accept suffering without retaliation. The nonviolent resister is one who is willing to accept violence if necessary but never to inflict it. He knows that undeserved suffering is redemptive.

Fifth, nonviolence avoids not only external physical violence but also internal violence of spirit. The nonviolent resister refuses both to shoot his opponent and to hate him. The principle of love stands at the center of nonviolence.

By love, King meant the love which has its root meaning in *agape*. He points out that *eros* is a sort of aesthetic or romantic love, while *philia* denotes a kind of reciprocal love. The person loves because he is loved. But to speak of love which enables one to love one's opponent, one cannot speak of *eros* or *philia*. It is agape which means understanding, redeeming goodwill for all men. This love is of God and it operates in the human heart. It is a disinterested love, loving for the sake of others. *Agape* is the love which seeks to preserve and to create community. It is a willingness to forgive seventy times seven to restore community. Agape is a recognition of the fact that all life is interrelated. In the light of this kind of love, all humanity is involved in one single process, and all men are brothers. To be commanded to love is to be commanded to restore community, to resist injustice, and to meet the needs of others.[23]

Sixth, nonviolent resistance is based on the conviction that the universe is on the side of justice. Hence, the believer in nonviolence has deep faith in the future. This enables him to accept suffering without retaliation. He knows that in his struggle for justice he has "cosmic companionship." King acknowledged that all who hold such faith do not believe in God but all may accept the fact that there is a creative force in the universe bringing all the disconnected aspects of reality into a harmonious whole.

King's nonviolent philosophy was in stark contrast to that of the creation and purpose of the White Citizens Councils. Their methods were of open and covert terror, brutal intimidation, and threats of starvation to the blacks. The aim of their boycotts was to impress and to destroy their victims if possible. They were organized to perpetuate injustice.

Although King accepted the leadership of the MIA unhesitatingly in public, in private he had some reservations. He felt that the apparent apathy among the black ministers presented a special problem. He said that he saw how jealousies, opportunism, and apathy corrode noble undertakings in the black community. King doubted whether he could depend upon his fellow ministers for support. In a soliloquy to find a moral and Christian basis for the Montgomery Bus Boycott, King concluded that they would use the method to give birth to justice and freedom and also to urge men to comply with the law of the land.[24]

The Role of the Black Church

Kings inaugural address as president of the Montgomery Improvement Association was delivered in the Holt Street Church before television cameras. Before he spoke, the crowd sang "Onward Christian Soldiers," and Reverend W. F. Alford, minister of Beulah Baptist Church, followed with prayer. Scriptures was read by Reverend U. J. Fields, minister of Bell Street Baptist Church. Martin Luther King then stood behind the pulpit.

As president of the MIA, King delivered a speech militant enough to arouse his followers to positive action and yet moderate enough to keep them controlled within Christian bounds. His dilemma was to make them courageous enough to fight for their cause and at the same time to tone down their hostility and resentment for their white oppressors. In his message, he strongly emphasized the doctrine of love. He insisted that their actions should be guided by the deepest principles of their Christian faith. Love was the regulating ideal.[25] Quoting from Booker T. Washington, King said that they should "never allow anyone to pull them so low as to make them hate him."[26] At the end of his address, King thanked God silently for the people's enthusiasm and positive response to his message.

As the struggle continued, the guiding principle was referred to as nonviolent resistance, noncooperation, and passive resistance. Pondering, King said that he had come to recognize early that the Christian doctrine of love, operating through the Gandhian method of nonviolence, was one of the most potent weapons available to blacks in the struggle for freedom.[27] Nonviolent resistance emerged as the Movement's primary technique. Love remained as the regulating ideal; that is, the spirit and motivation was furnished by Jesus Christ, but the method was that of Gandhi. Without the aid of the regular mass meetings held in various black churches of the city, the Movement would have been unable to spread its philosophy with the necessary speed to keep it alive. There was neither a black-owned radio station nor a widely read black newspaper in the area. By and large, the meetings were nonviolent in spirit. A favorite scripture passage was, "And now abideth faith, hope and love, these three; but the greatest of these is love" (I Cor. 13:13). For the mass-meeting audiences, the scriptural admonitions took on an immediate and personal meaning.

In his weekly remarks, King would stress the impractical and immoral use of violence. He told them that violence and toughness begets a greater toughness. Therefore, forces of hate should be met with the power of love. Physical force must be met with soul force, for the aim is never to defeat or humiliate the white man but to win his friendship and his understanding.

Strength of the Boycott

The Executive Board of the MIA appointed a committee of twelve to meet with the bus officials in Montgomery. King was chosen as spokesman, and it was his task to present three proposals:

1. a guarantee of courteous treatment on the bus
2. passengers to be seated on a first-come first-serve basis blacks sitting from the back
3. employment of black bus drivers on predominantly black routes.

In the glow of television lights, Mayor W. A. Gayle called the conference together. No agreement was reached at that meeting. However, the Mayor asked that a few members of the black delegation remain for a further session with the bus company officials. The group was smaller. The press was gone, and King was optimistic concerning progress. But his optimism ended when Jack Crenshaw, attorney for the bus company said that if they granted the blacks such demands they would go about boasting of a victory that they won over the white people. The white folks would not stand for that.[28] King asked the attorney to state specifically what his company was prepared to offer the blacks. Crenshaw replied that his company was willing to guarantee courtesy. The seating arrangements could not be changed because it would necessitate the violation of the law. As far as the bus drivers were concerned, his company had no intention then or later to hire "niggas."

Sometime later, Dr. King recalled that the whole experience enabled him to see that no one gives up privileges without a strong resistance. He also became aware that the real purpose of segregation was to oppress and to exploit the segregated. It was to perpetuate injustice and inequality.

At another official meeting, Dr. Frazier, outspoken segregationist of the Methodist Church, made it clear that he felt the Bus Boycott was wrong. And it was more wrong because ministers of the gospel led the protest. He maintained *in addition* that the minister's job was to lead the souls of men to God and not to get entangled in transitory social problems.[29] King, unable to contain his criticism, replied that they also knew the Jesus the minister mentioned. They experienced him and believe fully in the revelation of God in Jesus Christ. And therefore, they saw no conflict between their devotion to Jesus and their social action, because the gospel of Jesus Christ is personal as well as social.[30] King concluded that the Christian's ultimate allegiance should be to God rather than to the folkways of man. The meeting ended, and again no settlement was reached.

At the next meeting, a spokesman for the white establishment accused Dr. King of being the chief stumbling-block to a real solution of the problem. The accusation angered and embittered King. He confessed how he allowed himself to become angry and to lose control of himself. What he said, he said in haste, without thinking as he should.[31] He turned on himself and warned himself never to become bitter, no matter how emotional his opponents were. He was to maintain his composure.[32] Communications broke down at that meeting, and no other meeting was scheduled. The Men of Montgomery- a white businessmen organization made a further attempt to reopen negotiations. The boycott was hurting their business. After two trials, their efforts to reach a settlement failed because of the recalcitrance of the city fathers.

The city fathers failed to divide the blacks, and so they tried to divide the leaders. Black ministers were urged by prominent white citizens to oust Martin Luther King as leader of the Movement. Ostensibly their reason was that any other leader would effect a quicker and desired settlement for the Movement.

When word reached King that the whites sought to oust him as leader of the MIA, he began to think there was some truth in what the white citizens were saying. After three troubled nights, he reached the decision to resign. He submitted the names of two men whom he felt were dedicated to the cause and were prepared to continue the struggle in Montgomery. Meanwhile, the dejected leader assured the Executive Board that he would be active in the background. The Board rejected his resignation and gave him a unanimous vote of confidence.

"The powers that be" in Alabama would not be defeated. The city fathers this time announced in the local newspaper that a settlement was reached. The new terms were:

1. a guarantee of courtesy
2. a white- reserved section at the front of the bus, a black-reserved section at the rear, and a first-served and unreserved middle section
3. special all-black buses during the rush hours

The *Montgomery Advertiser* planned to publish the news on Sunday, January 22, but the Associated Press ran the story on Saturday, January 21. Carl T. Rowan, black editorial writer of the *Minneapolis Tribune* caught the story and called King at 8 p.m. to verify the agreement. Fortunately for the Movement, the news story broke on Saturday evening. Ministers were urged to announce in their Sunday morning worship service that the protest was still on. That Saturday night, King and a group of workers toured the black nightclubs and taverns to inform those there of the false rumor concerning the protest. The hoax finally failed.

The mayor, appearing on television, denounced the boycott. Simultaneously the three commissioners made it known that they had become members of the White Citizens Council. A series of arrests followed. Blacks were arrested for minor and often imaginary traffic violations. Blacks driving in the organized car pool were questioned about their licenses, insurance, and place of employment. They were told by policemen that there was a law against hitchhiking and were warned that they would be arrested for vagrancy if found wandering in white neighborhoods.

King was arrested for the first time and placed behind prison bars. The news of his arrest spread quickly through the black community in Montgomery. A number of blacks made their way to the city jail. Ralph Abernathy paid Kings cash bond, and one of King's deacons drove him home.

Once at home, King began to receive threatening telephone calls and letters. He became fearful for his safety. So affected was he that at one meeting he found himself saying if they found him sprawled out dead one day he did not wish them to fight back. He did not wish even his death to cause them to engage in a single act of violence. Rather, his wish was that should he die they should continue the protest with the same dignity and discipline already shown.[33] The threats continued, and they led King to the point of giving up the whole struggle. But one day in the kitchen of his house, he prayed aloud and experienced the presence of God assuring and encouraging him to stand up for righteousness and truth. King's uncertainty disappeared and he was prepared to face the enemy.

When King's house was bombed, his nonviolence was put to the test. It faced the immediate possibility of being transformed into violence. Hundreds of blacks gathered in front of King's destroyed home. In the crowd a black was reported to have told a policeman that "you have your 38, and I have mine. Let's battle it out." But King pleaded to the crowd to remain calm, to take their weapons home, and to love their white brothers. Following that destructive incident, members of King's church urged him to hire a personal bodyguard and an armed watchman for his house. He yielded to their request and applied for a license to carry a gun. He was refused the permit. King, meanwhile, could not reconcile the leader of a nonviolent cause keeping on his person a weapon of violence for protection. He remembered what Jesus said about the sword, that he who lives by the sword must die by the sword (Matt. 26: 52). As a result, King decided to get rid of the one weapon he owned.

The multiplicity of King's new responsibilities caused him to neglect his pastoral duties. He became only a Sunday preacher. He agreed that his church shared him willingly with the community. They gave of their own resources of time and purse into the struggle.[34]

Still seeking relentlessly to break the back of the Bus Boycott, the city fathers called the Montgomery County Grand Jury on February 13, 1956, to determine whether the boycott was a violation of the city law. The jury found the boycott illegal and more than one hundred persons were indicted. King's name was on the list. At the time of the indictments, King was at Fisk University, Nashville, giving a series of lectures. When he heard of the indictments, he terminated his lectures and returned to Montgomery. Martin Luther King, Sr., tried, without success, to convince his son, Martin, Jr., not to return to Montgomery.

Upon his arrival in Montgomery, King was greeted by television cameras and members of the press. Accompanied by his father and Ralph Abernathy and followed by a number of his church members, King hurried to the jail to be fingerprinted and photographed. His trial was set for March 19, 1956. On that day, friends and ministers from as far north as New York were present at the courthouse. Reporters representing publications in the United States, India, France and England were there to cover the proceedings.

William F. Thetford, the state's solicitor, attempted to prove that King disobeyed a law by organizing an illegal boycott. The attorneys for the defense- Arthur Shores, Peter Hall, Ozell Billingsley, Fred Cray, Charles Langford, and Robert Carter- argued that the prosecution failed to produce sufficient evidence to prove its case against King.

On Thursday afternoon, March 22, Judge Carter gave his verdict. King was declared guilty of violating the state's anti boycott law.[35] King was fined $500.00 and court costs, or 386 days at hard labor in the County of Montgomery. Friends signed King's bond, and the lawyers notified the judge that the case would be appealed.

King declared later that he sympathized with Judge Carter in his dilemma. For in convicting the leader of the boycott, Carter faced the condemnation of the nation and world opinion. To acquit the defender, he also faced the condemnation of the local community and those who kept him in office. In his verdict, Judge Carter convicted not only King but also every black in Montgomery.

Every effort to disunite the Movement only served to strengthen the unity. King observed that the opposition failed because it was unaware of with whom it dealt. Its methods were geared to the "old blacks," but they were fighting the "new blacks"- blacks who had been freed from fear.

The Opened Door

Finally, the MIA filed a suit in the United States Federal District Court requesting an end to the bus segregation on the grounds that it was contrary to the Fourteenth Amendment Further, the court was asked by the MIA to stop the city commissioners from violating the civil rights of black motorists and pedestrians. After three weeks of deliberations, a two-to-one decision was declared on June 4, 1956, that the city bus segregation laws of Alabama were unconstitutional. Judge Lynn, of Birmingham, dissented. The attorneys for the city announced that they would appeal the decision to the United States Supreme Court.

During this time, Reverend U.J. Fields became a problem to the Movement. He resigned as recording secretary of the MIA and accused the officers of misusing the funds.[36] The blacks began to classify him a "fool" and a "black Judas." A group of his own church met and voted him out as pastor. Later, however, he was reinstated. Fields regretted his action, and with courage, he rescinded his statement at a mass meeting held in the Beulah Baptist Church.

Attendants at the meeting were in no hurry to forgive Fields, but Dr. King reminded them of their commitment to nonviolence and that nonviolence also meant the avoidance of internal violence of spirit. He quoted the words of Christ: "He that is without sin among you, let him first cast a stone at her" (John 8:7). Then he recited the parable of the prodigal son and asked if they would be as the unforgiving brother, or in the spirit of Christ, follow the example of the loving and forgiving father. Fields was forgiven.

Meanwhile the car pool arrangement was falling apart. Liability insurance on wagons was being cancelled, and the city was taking legal action against the car pool itself. The hearing was set for Tuesday, November 13. The city's petition was directed against the MIA, several churches and individuals. The city alleged that the car pool was a "public nuisance" and a "private enterprise" operating without license fee or franchise. As the proceedings continued, news reached the court stating that the United States Supreme Court affirmed the decision of a special three-judge U.S. District Court in declaring Alabama's state and local laws requiring segregation on buses unconstitutional. One bystander said that the Almighty God spoke from Washington, D.C.[37]

A total of 8,000 men and women gathered around the two churches where meetings were simultaneously held to call off the protest. At the opening of one of the meetings, the Reverend Bob Graetz, a courageous white minister, read from Paul's letter to the Corinthians. When he concluded, "And now abideth faith, hope, love; but the greatest of these is love" (1 Cor. 13: 13), the people made a spontaneous outburst. King was confident then that, through all its difficulties, nonviolence had won its way into their hearts.[38]

A series of mass meetings followed to prepare the blacks for integrated buses. The prevailing theme was that the blacks should not regard the integrated buses as a victory over the white man. It was a victory for justice and democracy. Teaching sessions were arranged to tutor the people in nonviolent techniques. Leaflets on "Suggestions for Integrating Buses" were mimeographed and distributed throughout the city. On December 20, the bus integration order reached Montgomery, and subsequently a mass meeting was held to give the blacks last instructions before returning to the buses.

The supporters met at the St. John A. M. E. Church. There, in King's carefully prepared message, he said that they kept on with the faith that God was with them in the struggle. The long arc of the moral universe was bending in the direction of justice. They lived under the agony and darkness of Good Friday but with eager and certain expectation for the Easter Sunday morning glow. They witnessed how truth was crucified, and they saw goodness placed in the grave to rest. Nonetheless, they kept on with the strong conviction and undying hope that truth crushed to earth will one day rise again.[39]

King was one of the first blacks to ride the integrated buses. On that historic day a number of other black ministers also rode on the integrated buses throughout the city during the rush hour. The Montgomery bus integration triggered a series of bombings. Homes and churches were the targets. Yet victory for democracy and justice was secure, and it led to the formation of the Southern Christian Leadership Conference (SCLC) with headquarters in Atlanta, Georgia. Dr. King was elected president.

Looking back, King said that when he went to Montgomery as pastor he did not have the slightest idea he would become involved in a crisis in which nonviolent resistance would be applicable. He neither began a protest or even suggested one. He simply responded to the call of the people for a spokesman.[40] King reported that as he lived through the actual experience of the protest nonviolence became more than a method to which he gave intellectual assent. It became a commitment to a way of life. Many of the aspects that had not been cleared intellectually as regards nonviolence became solved for him in the area of practical action. A series of successful Bus Boycotts in Tallahassee, Atlanta, and other cities in the South followed the Montgomery boycott. The nonviolent technique was proving to be a powerful weapon in the black's struggle for justice. Following a trip to India, King decided to devote more time to the SCLC. He resigned as pastor of the Dexter Avenue Baptist Church on January 24, 1960. He moved his family to Atlanta and served as assistant minister to his father at the Ebenezer Baptist Church.

On February 1, 1960, a college student, Joseph McNeil, and three friends began a sit-in at the Woolworth store in Greensboro, North Carolina. The sit-in technique was started by a group called the Congress of Racial Equality (CORE). This organization was founded in 1943. The initial incident at Woolworth's touched off a gigantic sit-in movement among college students in North Carolina and across the South. The students preferred going to jail to paying fines. Sit-ins spread from department stores to supermarkets, theaters, and libraries. By 1961, one or more lunch counters in 108 Southern communities had desegregated.

A conference for the student sit-in leaders was held at Shaw University in Raleigh, North Carolina. There Dr. King emphasized the philosophy of nonviolence. At that conference, the Student Nonviolent Coordinating Committee (SNCC) was born. They used nonviolent techniques, but they did not seek the friendship of the segregationists. SNCC wanted power, a feeling shared by the membership of CORE. Under CORE, SNCC and SCLC leadership, the Freedom Riders were successful in getting the Interstate Commerce Commission to reaffirm its original ruling that segregation on buses and in bus stations was unlawful.

During the struggle in Albany, Georgia, King vowed to remain in jail until the blacks there received justice. He demanded integration of public facilities, the hiring of black policemen and firemen, and the black's full participation in the life of Albany. Misled, King allowed himself to be bailed out too soon. The blacks won nothing in Albany.

In Birmingham, the issues were four:

1. desegregation of lunch counters, restrooms, fitting rooms and drinking fountains in variety and department stores
2. upgrading and hiring of blacks on a nondiscriminatory basis throughout the business and industrial community of Birmingham
3. dropping all charges against jailed demonstrators
4. the creation of a biracial committee to work out a suitable timetable for desegregation in other areas of Birmingham's life.

The experience gained in the Montgomery Bus Boycott and the defeat suffered in Albany contributed to the extreme caution and careful planning for the Birmingham Movement. Wyatt Walker was sent to "spy out the land" and to lay the ground work for an intensive boycott. He checked on the city code of picketing and demonstration, gathered information on the bail bond situation, scheduled workshops on nonviolent techniques, and familiarized himself with downtown Birmingham.

During March and April, 1963, the election and the eventual runoff vote hindered the strategy of the boycott. In the meantime, King sought the support of key persons across the nation as an adequate preparation for the difficult days ahead. The boycott began with sit-ins. The main target was the business community. A total of sixty-five mass meetings were held in various black churches while the struggle lasted. The meetings were to keep the people informed, to hold them together, and to remind them of their commitment to the philosophy of nonviolence. At the end of each meeting, persons were challenged to join the army of nonviolence. Many responded.

Martin Luther King, Jr. called it a special army with no supplies but sincerity. Its uniform was determination; its arsenal, faith; and its currency, conscience. It was an army whose allegiance was only to God. Each volunteer was required to sign a commitment card which contained the pledge and the ten commandments of the nonviolent movement. They were based on Christian principles; for example, the first commandment was a pledge to meditate daily on the teachings of Jesus. The third was to walk and talk in the manner of love, for God is love. The fifth was to sacrifice personal wishes in order that all men might be free. The seventh was to seek to perform regular service for others and for the world. The eighth was to refrain from the violence of fist, tongue or heart. The ninth was to strive to be in good spiritual and bodily health. The tenth was to follow the direction of the Movement and of the captain on a demonstration.

King regretted that they did not have a sympathetic and understanding national press in Birmingham as they did in Montgomery and Albany. In Birmingham he was regarded as an outsider and, as such, incapable of leading the struggle there. King's response was that no black, in fact no American of the Republic to aid the cause of freedom and justice was an outsider. It was at that time when Martin pleaded for the projection of strong, firm leadership by the black ministers. King believed that the minister was freer, and more independent than any in the community and that his guidance, support and inspiration were necessary to lead the blacks to freedom.[41]

Simultaneously, blacks staged kneel-ins at white churches and at the library, and they marched on the country building to mark the opening of a voter registration drive. On Good Friday, April 12, 1963, King himself disobeyed the law in the spirit of Thoreau's Civil Disobedience and voluntarily submitted to arrest. In the Birmingham jail he wrote a letter to a group of white fellow clergymen who called the boycott "unwise and untimely." In his letter, King pointed out that in any nonviolent campaign four basic steps are followed:

1. collection of facts
2. negotiation
3. self-purification
4. direct action.

King made it known that the black leaders sought to negotiate with the city fathers, but the city fathers refused to engage in good-faith negotiation. Therefore, the blacks had no other alternative than to lay their cause before the conscience of the local community.

The jailed leader said that he earnestly opposed violent tension but that he believed in a type of constructive nonviolent tension which was necessary for growth. He referred to the civil disobedience of Shadrach, Meshach and Abednego in their refusal to obey Nebuchadnezzar's laws. He reminded them of the early Christians who were willing to face angry lions and chopping blocks rather than to submit to certain unjust laws of the Roman Empire. Then after referring to the appalling silence of "good people" on the issues at hand, King said that he was grateful to God that through the influence of the black church the way of nonviolence became an integral part of the struggle.[42]

On Friday, May 10, 1963, an agreement was reached on the four issues. It was another nonviolent victory for justice. The segregationist's reaction to this was generally the same as it was in Montgomery about eight years before. There were bombings of homes, bars, and churches, and innocent blacks were beaten.

As early as January, 1941, A. Philip Randolph, president of the Brotherhood of Sleeping Car Porters, called for 100,000 blacks to march on Washington in a massive demonstration against racial discrimination in industry. The march never materialized, but the threat of such an action was sufficient to cause President Roosevelt to issue an executive order establishing a committee on Fair Employment Practices. The events of the 1963 summer required an appropriate climax, and A. Philip Randolph proposed a march on Washington to unite the forces along the far-flung front.

On August 28, 1963, nearly 250,000 persons of all walks of life journeyed to the nation's capital. King rejoiced that one significant element of the march was the participation of the white churches. King announced that the march on Washington was endorsed officially by the National Council of the Churches of Christ in the U.S.A, the American Baptist Convention, the Brethren Church, the United Presbyterian Church in the U.S.A., and by thousands of congregations and ministers of the Lutheran and Methodist churches.[43] Cardinal Spellman of New York called for accelerated activity on racial justice.

In Boston, Cardinal Cushing named eleven priests as representatives to the occasion. Virtually every major Jewish organization endorsed the march. Dr. Joachim Prinz, president of the American Jewish Congress, was one of' the day's chairmen. King noted that the march was the first organized black operation which was accorded respect and coverage of the media commensurate with its importance.

Standing dwarfed by the brooding statue of Abraham Lincoln, King proclaimed his dream with conviction. He said that he had a dream. That one day on the red hills of Georgia, the sons of former slaves and the sons of former slave owners would be able to sit down together at the table of brotherhood. They would be able to speed up that day when all God's children would be able to join in the words of the old Negro spiritual: "Free at last! Free at last! Thank God Almighty-Free at last!"[44]

In June of 1963, Martin Luther King, made a coast-to-coast speaking tour. He addressed 25,000 in Los Angeles, 10,000 in Chicago. On June 23, 1963, King led 125,000 people in a great Freedom Walk in Detroit. The Civil Rights leader marched side by - side with Walter P. Reuther, president of' the United Auto Workers and the Reverend C. L. Franklin, chairman of the Detroit Council of Human Rights, which sponsored the event. King met a different type of black in the North and West; they were not concerned about nonviolent actions. They cheered loudly when King spoke of violence- but only to make a point for nonviolence. As King spoke of the power of nonviolence to disarm the opponent, they laughed.[45] The blacks' problem in Chicago was the inadequate and segregated school system of the city. They demanded the replacement of public school superintendent, Benjamin C. Willis. Coupled with Willis' replacement was the demand for a better housing system in the ghetto.

In Watts, King observed that black unemployment was higher than in the Great Depression. The blacks also suffered from discriminatory housing laws. King saw these conditions to be so serious as to alter the blacks' Freedom Movement. He believed that any mass violence by the blacks to secure justice would hinder and defeat the ultimate cause of freedom. The constant question in his mind was whether the Movement would change from nonviolence to violence where there was that solid manipulation which mocked empty-handed petition.

King feared that reason would be replaced by rage. White leadership in the North relied too often and too much on the patience of the blacks, on substitutes, and on tokens. King saw the end of Northern whites' crutches to keep Northern blacks in check. It was only a question of "how long."[46]

In listing the achievements of the nonviolent method, Dr. King wrote that the 1960 sit-ins desegregated lunch counters in more than 150 cities within a year. The 1961 Freedom Riders put an end to segregation in the interstate travel. The 1956 Bus Boycott in Montgomery, Alabama, brought to an end the segregation on the buses not only of that city but in nearly every city of the South. The 1963 Birmingham Movement and the climactic March on Washington won passage of the most powerful Civil Rights Law in a century. The Selma Movement brought enactment on the Voting Rights Law. The nonviolent marches in Chicago brought about a new housing agreement.[47]

The End of the Trail

The Southern Christian Leadership Conference staff in Atlanta delegated the leader of the Civil Rights Movement to go to Washington for the Poor People's Campaign and specified that he should go by way of Memphis. King's stop in Memphis was to assist the garbage collectors who were demanding a recognition of their union by the city, and a 60-cents-per-hour raise.

Before leading the march in Memphis, King scheduled a series of rallies in the city. The first and only was held on the evening of April 3, 1968, at the Mason Street Temple. King stepped to the pulpit for his last time. It was a rainy night, but some 2,000 spirited followers were present. As King's address gained momentum, he said it did not matter to him anymore because he had gone to the mountain top and had seen the promised land. In joyful lamentation he said he may not get there with those who would reach the land. But he wished them to know they will get there. The Civil Rights leader said he was feeling happy. He was not worrying about anything. He was not fearing any man. And then he thundered out the words that his eyes had seen the glory of the coming of the Lord.[48] The next day, Thursday, April 4, 1968, at 7:05 p.m., the Civil Rights leader was pronounced dead by Dr.

Jerry Francisco, Memphis coroner. Martin Luther King, Jr. was felled by an assassin's bullet.

Sam Donaldson interviewed Martin Luther King, Sr. on ABC's "Nightline" Thursday, August 25, 1983. King, Sr. said that as a boy of about eight to ten years old his son Martin would tell his mother that when he grew up to be a man he would turn the world around. The child said that he would let the people do it for him. But as he was maturing, Martin began to tell his parents that what he felt he had to do, and that was the greatest, was to give his life.

3

The Church and The Civil Rights Movement

This chapter investigates King's concept of the church and its mission. Attempts are made to ascertain what biblical symbol or model he held of the church. Special attention is given to any event which might have been significant in altering his understanding of the church.

A major difficulty in writing about Martin Luther King's view of the church is that he has no systematic statement as to its nature. He says almost nothing about ecclesiology in terms of its constitution and ordinances. He appears to have accepted the traditional policy of the black church. He laid great stress on the social mission of the church, however, and his view of the church as the Body of Christ gave sanction to his social concerns.

In the New Testament, there are a number of symbols for the church. For example, the Flock of God (Acts 20:28) emphasizes the need to care for the church. The bride symbol (Eph. 5:25-26) presents the church in expectation and stresses its eschatological nature. The Temple of God (Eph. 2:21, Rev. 3:12) denotes the church as the place where God dwells. There, God is revealed and worshipped. The temple idea is also the visible continuing incarnation of Christ. The People of God expression (1 Pet. 2:9) explains the church as a people called out to represent God here on earth. The Body of Christ designation of the church (Eph. 1:22-23; Rom. 12:5; I Cor. 12:12) signifies the missionary and social activities. Jesus in his own body preached the gospel to the poor; healed the broken-hearted; preached deliverance to the captives and set men free (Luke 4:18). In the meanwhile, the ecumenical role of the church is embodied in this symbol of the church.

Alan Richardson describes the church as the means of Christ's work in the world. She is his hands, feet, mouth and voice. The church, therefore, has a serious responsibility of being a servant, not only to speak of God's love but also to act it out in village streets, in cities, and in county jails.[49]

Martin Luther King opted for the Body of Christ as the most meaningful symbol of the church and her mission today. In a written reply from the Birmingham city jail to fellow white ministers, King affirmed that he loved the church and saw the church as the Body of Christ.[50] Continuing, he deplored the church's nonconcern for social issues. In the midst of the difficult struggle to rid the nation of racial and economic injustice, he heard pastors say that the gospel had no real concern for social issues.[51] The Civil Rights leader noticed that many churches committed themselves instead to an otherworldly religion which, he said, made a strange, un-Biblical distinction between body and soul, between the secular and the sacred.[52] King believed that human progress came not as a matter of mere inevitability, for it is achieved through the tireless efforts of' men willing to be co-workers with God.[53]

King revealed that his commitment to the ministry of' Jesus Christ, and therefore being a member of the Body of Christ, left him no choice but to speak up for the weak, the voiceless, and the victims in America.[54] His total commitment to Christ convinced him that if none else spoke out those who made up the Body of Christ were compelled to speak for them and to raise the questions they could not raise for themselves.[55] But the Body must also suffer. It was a reality to King that the chief purpose of the Christian Church is the salvation of individuals.[56] He was totally convinced that there is an element of God in every man, so that no matter how low one sinks into racial bigotry, he can be redeemed through suffering love.[57] In a speech delivered in the summer of 1967, Martin Luther King avowed that they would match the enemies capacity to inflict suffering with a capacity to endure suffering. He gave notice that they would meet physical force with what he called "soul force." Ultimately, and soon he felt, their capacity to suffer would wear down the enemies. And therefore, they would win their freedom. The goal was not only to win their freedom but to win the enemies over as friends by appealing to their hearts and consciences through their suffering.[58] King's faith was in the inner spiritual "church"- that is, the body of Christ within the institutional Church, the true Ecclesia and hope of the world.[59]

The Body of Christ metaphor suggests the interrelatedness of the parts of the body. Every part is necessary for the proper functioning of the whole. Each is bound up with the other so that when one member suffers, the whole body suffers. King had an opportunity to commend a few ministers of the gospel of Christ and rabbis of the Jewish faith for their fortitude in the face of threats, intimidations, and physical danger to declare the Fatherhood of God and the brotherhood of men.[60] The Reverend Dr. King believed that the Church in America was presented with an amazing challenge and responsibility to allow the spirit of Christ to work toward the molding of a genuine Christian nation.[61] If the church would do that with devotion and valor, King envisioned the time when men everywhere would recognize that they are one in Christ Jesus.[62]

King had a peculiar feeling of security and motivation when he was supported by clergymen of different denominations.[63] He always welcomed opportunities to share in services and conferences other than Baptist. For example, King participated in an ecumenical conference sponsored by the Massachusetts Council of Churches and at St. John's Seminary, a Jesuit school.[64] He attended the world convention of the Disciples of Christ in San Juan.[65] King delivered an address at the General Assembly of the Unitarian-Universalist Association meeting in Hollywood. There he stated that the black man was freer than he was a decade ago. Yet he was not totally free. He was able to enjoy more dignity than he ever did in America, but he was not yet equal with his white brothers.[66] And at New York's Riverside Church, King spoke passionately decrying the cruel irony of black and white soldiers fighting and dying together for a nation that has been unable to seat them together in the same schools.[67]

It must not pass unnoticed that the Civil Rights leader had experiences of disappointment with a large number of white ministers, priests, and rabbis of the South. He expected and relied upon their support, but they were outright opponents to the freedom movement. King complained that he went to Birmingham filled with the hope that the white religious leadership of the area would sympathize with the justice of the cause. With deep moral concern he imagined them serving as channels through which grievances would reach up to the power structure. But he had a very disappointing experience.[68] Martin Luther King knew that it took more than the denominational church to oppose and overcome the evils of social injustice in America. Furthermore, he believed strongly in the One God who is Lord of the Church, and the Father of all Mankind.[69]

Recalling the cooperation of the churches during the Montgomery Bus Boycott, King noted that the speakers represented various denominations and thus removed any grounds for sectarian jealousy. In an expression of gratefulness and pleasure King recalled that the big blessing of the Montgomery movement was that Baptists, Methodists, Lutherans, Presbyterians, Episcopalians and others united with a determination to rise above denominational lines. King mentioned also that although no leaders of the Roman Catholic Church joined the protest, many of their congregations got involved. All stood hand in hand in the bond of Christian love.[70]

James H. Cone, Professor of Theology at Union Theological Seminary in New York, considers the church as that community which refuses to accept the status quo and protests continuously against the oppression and humiliation of man. The church can be, therefore, the movement through which those oppressed express their will to the world. Hence, Cone had no difficulty in seeing the church as a liberating agency whose chief concern is to be to the world that visible hope of God's intention for humanity.[71] In his writings, the Civil Rights leader was careful to mention the firmness and boldness of the early church in a stance against the evils of the time. To King, the early Christians rejoiced at being deemed worthy to suffer for what they believed. He noted that in every town they entered, the authorities became disturbed and treated the Christians as disturbers of the peace and outside agitators. Nevertheless, the Christians kept on in the conviction that they were "a colony of heaven," called to obey God rather than men. Their number and material resources were small, but their commitment was large. Continuing, the crusader for Civil Rights warned, challenged, and rejoiced that the early Christians could not be astronomically intimidated because they were too God-intoxicated.[72] Through the effort and example of the Christians, the ancient evils of infanticide and gladiatorial contests were brought to an end.[73]

Martin Luther King believed the church should work with passionate determination to solve the racial problem. He emphasized that it was always the church's responsibility to broaden horizons, question the status quo and to break with mores when necessary.[74] The Civil Rights leader argued that it was not enough for religious institutions to be active in the realm of ideas only. He believed strongly that the church ought not remain silent and unconcerned behind the anesthetizing security of stained-glass windows when social evils are rampant in the community. It was urgent and obligatory to King that the church move into areas of housing and education to hasten the liberation of the black man.[75]

Further, Martin Luther King refused to accept the finality of ideological conflict engendered by the relativism of his day. King felt that faith in God could transcend the opposing relativism and effect reconciliation. He saw faith as the power of reconciliation which operated to unite relative perspectives and thus eliminate ideological conflicts.[76] King believed that faith was the commitment of a man to resist any separation of man from man. It binds one to struggle against the attacks on the common good, against racism, discrimination and the brokenness of man's spiritual and intellectual life.[77] In this respect, Herbert Warren Richardson could regard King as a foremost proponent of a theology of reconciliation.[78]

In any discussion, faith's aim is agreement, not dialogue. In war, faith expects and works for peace. Faith seeks the common good in economic struggles and anticipates ecumenical union in churches working together. Relativism creates the gaps, but faith bridges them for a workable and meaningful unity. King's support of the United Nations, his creation of the Southern Christian Leadership Conference and his desire for peace and ecumenism were in keeping with his belief in the transcending and uniting power of faith. King saw God at work in those institutions.[79]

In the closing section of one of his sermons, King admitted that honesty impelled him to confess that transformed non-conformity could mean to walk down the valley of suffering, to lose a job, and to have a six-year-old daughter ask him why he had to go to jail so much.[80] King said that Christianity does not protect one from the pain and agony of mortal existence. For Christianity always insisted that the cross preceded the crown. King proclaimed, therefore, that to be a Christian, one must take up his cross with all its accompanying difficulties, agonies and tragedies and bear it until that same cross leaves its marks upon us and redeems us to that more excellent way which comes only through suffering.[81]

Martin Luther King, Jr., saw the church as dynamic, relevant and with a mission for his day and age. He was convinced the church had a significant role to play at that time chiefly because the issues were not only political but moral.[82] King concluded that the church had a responsibility of being the moral guardian of the community. Dr. King called for the church to be the "head-light" instead of the "tail-light" of social justice. He saw the religious community adjusted to the status quo as the end of the 20th century drew near. It stood sheltered and comfortable behind other community agencies when it should have been a beacon light guiding humanity on to higher levels of justice.[83] Those words rushed from the lips of the confused Civil Rights leader in April, 1963, in response to the disappointing support he received from the white ministers, priests, and rabbis of the South.

William B. McClain records that the black church was conceived in the womb of Africa and born in slavery in America.[84] Slave masters used it as an aggressive instrument of oppression. It became a tool of power to establish, sanction, reinforce, and internalize the false concept that blacks were subhuman and bastard children born of an illicit cohabitation between inferiors.

Early in the history of the black man and American Christianity, the blacks noticed a contradiction between the gospel of Christ and the system of slavery. They saw a contradiction between the spirit of the gospel and the claim of white supremacy. So the independent black church emerged as a protest against racial theology and racial ecclesiology of the Church in America.[85] The black Christians did not accept the white man's interpretation of the Christian faith. The independent black church became a protest center and an organizing base for slave revolts. Later, it became a welfare unit and agent of survival. Today, it is a liberating force in black culture.[86]

The organizations of the black church were much more than religious organizations. They were welfare and community centers for the social life of blacks.[87] They provided opportunities and activities in which free blacks could achieve social status and develop leadership ability among themselves.

A new type of religious leadership emerged in response to the changes in the religious life of the blacks. The secular outlook which resulted partly from a broader education and partly from a greater degree of sophistication with life, distinguished the new trend. Even many semi-literate religious leaders of smaller churches show the influence of secularization. The increasing concern of the black masses with the problems of employment, housing, and discrimination in the urban centers is demanding the minister's involvement. Hence, the black preacher is concerned with the rights of blacks.[88]

The black religious leader must move beyond "getting the Negro in Heaven" to "advancing the race" here on planet earth.[89] Black ministers have become especially interested and active in advising the blacks in the matter of voting. A number of ministers, like A. Clayton Powell, Jr., have merged their religious calling with the secular role of a political leader.[90] James H. Cone suggests that Garvey in the 1920's, the Black Muslims in the 1930's, Powell in the 1940's, King in the 1950's, and Malcolm X in the 1960's served to remind the black church of what its role in society ought to be.[91] The black church is being made to realize that blackness has a new content. It involves more than the color of the skin. It is to share in the existence of all those who are oppressed and to act toward their liberation.[92]

Martin Luther King, Jr., a pastor and the son and grandson of Baptist pastors, found it natural to regard the black church as the base of operation and inspiration for the Civil Rights Movement. In times of retreat, the Movement went to the church. The black church identified with the oppressed minority. It sought to serve the interest and needs of the oppressed caught up in a hostile environment.[93] From time immemorial, the black man in America was involved in a struggle for freedom, justice and manhood. The blacks had no protection from the law or the white church. Daily he was burdened with the problem of survival among a hostile people, in a hostile land amid oppressive conditions. Chief Justice Taney sealed the black's doom in a verdict given in the Dred Scott case. His verdict was that a black man had no rights that a white man was bound to respect.[94]

The black church, therefore, was the key instrument in the survival of black people. This accounts for the black's loyalty to it. For the black church enabled the blacks to survive, to function, and to maintain some degree of sanity and hope. Through the black church, serving not only as a religious aid but also as a social agency, the blacks were able to preserve some semblance of pride and self-respect. In such a society where the oppressed needed to vent their feelings, it was the black church which definitely provided for the blacks both an emotional outlet and a spiritual purgative.[95]

King emphasized that at the beginning of the protest movement in Montgomery, Alabama, the twice-a-week get-together at the black churches were indispensable channels of communication because Montgomery had neither a black owned radio station nor a widely read black newspaper.[96] He mentioned that the philosophy of nonviolence was disseminated mainly through the regular mass meetings which were held in the various black churches of the city.[97] The meetings were held from church to church.[98] The Civil Rights Leader felt that it was beyond doubt that the mass meetings held in the black churches accomplished on Monday and Thursday nights what the Christian Church had failed to accomplish on Sunday mornings.[99]

While the meetings began at seven in the evenings, the churches were often completely filled by five in the afternoons. Before the official meetings began, some early arrivals read books, while others joined in groups, singing the traditional songs which brought to mind the long history of the blacks' suffering. The meetings followed a simple pattern of songs, prayer, Scripture, opening remarks by the president, collection, reports from various committees and a "pep talk." This pattern is similar to the order of worship service in the black Baptist Church.[100] In his letter written in the Birmingham city jail, King expressed his gratefulness to God for the influence and backing of the black church. Through the black church the method of nonviolence became the integral part of the struggle for justice.[101]

King believed that the church was the chief moral guardian of the community and had an inescapable duty to teach men how to overcome evil intentions and to be good citizens. He held, therefore, that the church should exalt virtues of kindheartedness and conscientiousness.[102] He believed further that somewhere along the way the church must remind men that without intelligence, goodness and conscientiousness will become brutal forces leading to shameful crucifixions. Therefore, the church must not become tired of reminding men that they have a moral responsibility to be intelligent.[103]

The church should urge all her worshipers to develop a world perspective which would enable them to rise above their narrow provincialism and sectionalism; above racial prejudice, above the narrow confines of their personal concerns to the broader concerns of all humanity.[104] King warned that there were only two alternatives: to live together as brothers or to perish together as fools.[105] Quoting from John Donne, Martin Luther King stressed that "no man is an island." Each man is a piece of a continent; and each man dies in the death of every man.[106] Hence the church must make it clear that segregation is a moral evil which no Christian can accept. Segregation is wrong because it relegates persons to the status of things. It does something to the personality, and it damages the soul of men. Segregation gives the segregator a false sense of superiority and the segregated a false sense of inferiority. Likewise, the church can say to men everywhere that there is no superior race. Academically there may be superior or inferior individuals in all races, but no anthropologist would say that any race is superior. Through religious education, the church can tell the truth on these issues.[107]

Furthermore, the church has the moral responsibility to educate that the black is not inherently criminal but that it is poverty and ignorance which breed crime irrespective of the racial group. The church can reveal the true intention of the black. The black does not seek to dominate the nation politically; he does not aim to overthrow anything nor strive to upset the social structure but merely seeks to create a moral balance within the society. And, too, a few were beginning to believe that King was only seeking to clear a way for blacks to marry whites. He made the Movement's intentions clear in saying that the church could make plain the basic aim of the black man. The black man was in search of justice to be the white man's brother and not his brother-in-law.[108]

Martin Luther King suggested that the church can do much to open channels of communications between blacks and whites. King felt that the problem was ignorance brought about by separation. Men hate each other for the simple reason that they do not know each other. They cannot know each other because they are separated from each other.[109] In the same breath he said that the greatest tragedy to befall a society is to attempt to live in monologue instead of dialogue.

Geographically, the world is one. Through scientific and technological genius, man has made the world into one neighborhood. Now, the church faces an urgent challenge and fact through spiritual and moral commitments to make the world a brotherhood. Brotherhood and survival depend upon a true appreciation and acceptance of the interrelatedness of a people's dependence and interdependence on one another.[110] In the chapel of the Southern Baptist Theological Seminary, Louisville, Kentucky, King proclaimed that no individual or nation could live alone. He admonished that Christian gathering that it is God's wish that people live together on planet earth.[111] The Civil Rights Leader refused to accept the view that mankind was so tragically bound to what he called "a midnight without stars, but filled with racism and war that the bright daybreak of peace and brotherhood could not become a realized reality."[112]

In accepting the Nobel Peace Price, King warned that a way of peace was urgent. And it was a burden of all people of the world to find it to live together. Unless found in time nothing could stop the pending cosmic song of lamentation for the dead. King challenged the world to come up with a method for a lifestyle which would reject revenge and aggression and retaliation. He himself was convinced that the foundation for any such method could only be love- 'agape'.[113] King regarded the 1964 Nobel Prize for Peace as a burden of responsibility and a commission to work harder for the brotherhood of man.[114] He was fully aware that such commission took him beyond national allegiances. His commitment to the ministry of Jesus Christ, coupled with this new commission, plagued him to become a maker of peace.[115] This was why, in referring to America's enemies in North Vietnam, he could say that no human declaration could make the enemy less than a brother.[116] King predicted that one day somebody would tell us that even though there may be political and ideological differences between us, we have got to sit down together around the table of brotherhood, for the Vietnamese, the Russians and the Chinese are all our brothers. King thundered that he had a dream. In his dream he longed for the day when the empty stomachs of Mississippi would be filled, and brotherhood would be more than a few words at the end of a prayer. He wanted that to be the first order of business on every legislative agenda.[117]

As he concluded his chapel address at Southern Baptist Theological Seminary, King grieved that before the daybreak of brotherhood, some would get scarred up. Some, like the apostles Paul and Peter, would have to go to jail. Others would be called names and be misunderstood, misrepresented and misquoted.[118] And working toward a climax for enlistment and a faith commitment, Martin Luther King made it known that God is at work in the process, working through history for the salvation of man. "So with this faith we can move on."[119]

Martin Luther King explained that he could not remain silent on the Vietnam War for the following reasons: *First,* the motto of the SCLC is "To save the soul of America." He said that it should be incandescently clear that no one who had any concern for the integrity and life of America could ignore the war in Vietnam.[120] *Second,* he regarded the Nobel Peace Prize as a commission to work harder and more inclusively for "the brotherhood of men." However, King acknowledged that even if he were not the 1964 recipient of that prize, his calling and commitment to Jesus could lead him to no other conclusion than to take a stand against the war.[121] *Third,* as he traveled around the country preaching the philosophy of nonviolence, youngsters asked why America was using violence in Vietnam to effect social change if it were true that social change comes most meaningfully through nonviolent action.

King's exposure to the northern and western black ghettos caused him to realize the depth of poverty which existed in some sections of America. He noticed that the nation was spending some *$322,000* for each enemy killed while only about $53 was spent on each person classified as "poor" in the war on poverty at home. King said that the war narrowed the domestic welfare programs, and made the poor, both white and black, bear the heaviest burdens at the front and at home. He complained that the war was undermining the Civil Rights Movement and damaging domestic programs.[122]

In calling for an immediate end to the war in Vietnam, King gave an answer for Communism. It is a "true revolution of values" which sees individual capitalists of the West investing huge sums of money in Asia, Africa, and South America not only for their own profits but also for the betterment of those countries. King testified that a true revolution of values would take hold of the world order and say that war is not the just way to settle differences.[123]

Dr. King declared that wisdom gained through experience should tell us that war is absolete.[124] That was part of a Christmas, 1967, sermon delivered by King in Ebenezer Baptist Church, Atlanta, Georgia, and carried live over the CBC Network. He expounded that the very destructive nature of modern weapons of war eliminates even the possibility that war could serve as a negative good.[125] King referred to the conquerors of old who came killing in the quest for peace. He singled out Alexander, Julius Caesar, Charlemagne, and Napoleon. He included Hitler and saw where all were akin in seeking a peaceful world order, but all were failures.[126] The Baptist preacher mentioned the eloquent talk about peace by the present world leaders, but the bombs still fall in Vietnam. King propounded that peaceful ends must be pursued through peaceful means.[127]

Reasoning further, Dr. King suggested that if life is worth living, then, mankind has a right to survive.[128] Mankind must affirm the sacredness of all human life. Man is a child of God, made in God's image, and therefore must be respected as such. King was certain that not until men acknowledge this everywhere and nations believe this everywhere would there be an end to all wars.[129] Taking a faith stance, the 1964 Nobel Peace Prize winner spoke of his dream. War will come to an end. Men would transform their swords into plough shares and their spears into pruning hooks. Weapons of war will become machinery for agriculture. Nations would think of war no more. Mankind's chief concern then would be to preserve life and not to destroy life.[130]

King's stand on the Vietnam war brought him a great deal of criticism, and yet because of his resolute commitment to peace, he was constrained by some to run for president of the United States of America in 1968. But as early as April 25, 1967, at a news conference held at

Ebenezer Baptist Church in Atlanta, Dr. King spoke of what he knew and accepted his role to be. He saw his role as one which should operate outside the realm of party politics. His role was to raise the issues and, through action, create the situation which would cause whatever party in power to act creatively and constructively.[131]

In his weekly remarks as president of the Montgomery Improvement Association, King stressed that the aim of the Bus Boycott was never to defeat or humiliate the white man but to win his friendship and understanding.[132] King always regarded the white man either as a friend or as a potential friend. The ideological differences between the white and black man stood as obstacles to eventual reconciliation and friendship. But friendship—a change of attitude and behavior—would be the key to social justice.

Faith presented the hope that one day the invisible unity of mankind will become visible and actual as white and black men join in love, in holy communion and in one common goal and good.[133] Thus, the man with this faith—vision will return good for evil, nonviolence for violence. King stressed that nonviolence was the only practical way to resist evil, for the nonviolent stance was based on a true comprehension of reality. One ideology thrives on the opposition to it. The opposition strengthens that which it opposes in the effort of opposing it.

King's goal in the struggle against social evil was the total interrelatedness of man with man. King emphasized friendship as the ultimate value of human life. It was not his intention to defeat but to win friendship in the struggle. It was the firm belief of King that self-sacrificing love develops naturally out of friendship-love, which is a common relationship with the one who received good for the evil he inflicted. The Civil Rights Leader understood Christian love to be friendship, and he moved from friendship to brotherhood as the goal of all life.

This is in contrast with self-sacrificing love being the chief good of human life. This ethic must accept evil as indispensable and perhaps valuable to human life, for it is evil which necessitates a self-sacrificial act. Self-sacrifice is only good because it checks and deters the evil. In this context we can only know the good that is deterrent and not the good that is essential of selfsacrifice.[134] Reinhold Niebuhr reintroduced this Reformation but semi-Manichean concept of evil in American theology. King, however, repudiated the Niebuhrian posture and introduced his own understanding of evil. The Civil Rights Leader saw evil as the structure which engendered ideological conflicts. It was a structure which was to be opposed not by settling for proximate justice in the political order, and acknowledging the legitimacy of violent force to restrain evil but by striving for a holy community of love in this world by the nonviolent striving to overcome evil with good.[135]

Evil is conquered when the good it strives to overcome allows it to triumph. With the full application of the power of evil on the good, the good maintains a posture of inaction. But evil in its vigor and confidence refuses to note that inaction is action and at times much more powerful than action itself. For as the good remains in a fixed position of inaction receiving all the insults, cuts, bruises, and pains of death, silently she strikes with force, persistently and on target with mortal blows. The evil beats itself to death. Only the good, in allowing evil to overcome it, can and will overcome evil for good: that is, put an end to evil.

4

A Dream Deferred

The major thrusts of King's views of the church and its mission are evaluated. His method of nonviolence is examined along with a statement of his major contributions to the Civil Rights Movement. Finally, an attempt is made to classify Martin Luther King, Jr. as pastor and a prophet of social justice.

From the beginning of the Montgomery Bus Boycott in December, 1955, it was the teaching of Jesus in the Sermon on the Mount which inspired the blacks to launch a protest without violence. Later in the black man's fight for justice, the technique and philosophy of nonviolence were employed but love remained the "regulating ideal." The enemy was always the evil system, never the individual. The individual was the victim of the system, and he needed to be convinced of this fact to win him as a friend and brother.

The weapon of persuasion was not reason alone or brute force, but "soul force" and "suffering love." Gandhi believed that things of fundamental importance to a people are never obtained by reason alone. It was his conviction that such would have to be taken by their suffering.[136] This is suffering power. It is what some people may call "paying their dues." After the pain, which is the price, they claim what was rightfully their own. King concurred that suffering was infinitely more potent than coercion to convert the opponent and to open his ears which were closed otherwise to the voice of reason.

Gandhi understood "unmerited suffering" in terms of the law of *karma* which achieves salvation through the accumulation of merits. King's "undeserved suffering" was related to the Christian idea of brotherly love. He understood this as love flowing over and out to others in action and which sought nothing in return. This was his concept of God's love at work in the hearts of men.[137]

To match the sword with love and to oppose brutal force with Christian meekness can be a dangerous risk of human lives. Yet King believed it was less precarious than to fight violence with violence. Violence creates more social problems than it solves. Moral force becomes more potent than direct physical retaliation. King's path to freedom was not through inflicting violence but through suffering violence. Violence as a method has been tried repeatedly but only to fail miserably leaving the blacks in a worse state of bondage.

King strongly believed that although man has a propensity for good or evil, he eventually responds to the good. Thus he believed that even the worst segregationist could become an integrationist. King's strength was in his faith in man's ability to change. He refused to accept the evil system and to become entangled in the relativism of his day. His absolute faith in the American dream, which he felt was based in the justice of God, transcended the conflicting ideologies in the way of progress.

King rejected the method of political campaigns where one side would blast the other and positionize itself on a particular issue of tension to gain control over the other. It was not a case where one side survived only on the continuous mistakes of the other. For the target was not persons but the segregation laws, the evil system. The aim was to make the constitution fulfill its promise to the blacks of America. King relied heavily on the faith and goodwill of the black and white church of America to challenge and change the status quo through massive nonviolent protests. But if both churches were to fail him, King still had hope in the American dream that all men were created equal and endowed with inalienable rights. He believed that the universe was moral and that history was moving toward its just fulfillment. Behind the constitution and ahead of history, God stood pulling down every mountain of injustice. For King, the cause of freedom was not a wild dream, but a reality to be achieved in the history of this world.

Through the method of nonviolence, Martin Luther King made the greatest sacrifice in offering bodies to be beaten by policemen, tormented by dogs, and thrown into jail for disobeying unjust laws.

He laid lives bare to fatal shots from any gun triggered by the fear and insecurity of the opponent. King's own life was constantly threatened. Yet throughout the struggle he maintained a remarkable calmness and treated all men as brothers or potential brothers. Nonviolence was a planned method. Leaders of the Civil Rights Movement never went into any community or staged any protest without first examining the whole situation. Targets were definite and non-personal. The intent was to put justice in business and in community life.

A closer look at the method of nonviolence reveals that King used the institution which the white man tolerated the blacks to own—that is, the black church—and the induced fear of the live or die idea of humble nonresistance. They boomeranged and became potent in the blacks' liberation. As long as the blacks stayed within their church—"in their place"—and accepted the dictates of the white man, they were free within the bondage of segregation. But the "new blacks" realized that if they stood with their church in a nonviolent resistance protest of justice, they had a hope of being declared free throughout the length and breadth of America in accordance with the United States Constitution and the American dream.

Joseph H. Fichter writing in "American Religion and the Negro" said that the nonviolent movement came from the heart of the black church. He noted that the movement revitalized the black church and in addition gave the message of the church a relevant and reliable appeal.[138] The plans for the Movement were developed in the black church. All their strategy meetings were held in the institution the white man permitted them to own. When the white man came to realize this, he began to bomb and to destroy their churches. But it was too late. What was externalized had become internalized, and the church was no longer enclosed within the four walls for King and the blacks. It was out in the world, scattered and doing what it must do to save the dignity, personality, and "the soul of America." Furthermore, the struggle for liberation required the black church to become more of a movement than an institution. It moved the black church into avenues of controversy and into a maze of issues that the white church preferred to shun. But the issues of survival and the liberation of mankind and the world confront the white church as well as the black church. It too will need to become a movement committed to set the captives free.[139]

Dr. E. Stanley Frazier of the Methodist Church in Montgomery, Alabama, admonished the Civil Rights Leader, the Reverend Dr. King, that the job of the minister was to lead the souls of men to God rather than to become involved in transitory social problems. King spoke of his experiential knowledge of God as revealed in Jesus Christ and declared that true devotion to the religion of Jesus seeks to rid the earth of social evils. True religion is concerned with both the soul of men and the social and economic conditions which scar the soul. Hence the gospel is social and personal, the good news for man's present and future life.

Here one recalls Hegel's statement that religion should be humane and not other-worldly. It is popular, not confined to the men of the cloth. As a living power, religion should flourish in the life of a nation. It should be visible in the habits of its people. Religion should influence their ideals, customs, actions, and festivals. It should enliven their hearts, wills, deeds and imagination.[140] Professor Cone declared that the Biblical God is the God who is involved in the historical process for the purpose of human liberation.[141] To know him is to know what he is doing in historical events as they are related to the liberation of the oppressed. God is known as the one who acts in history liberating Israel from oppression. It is impossible for any to encounter Israel's Savior and still remain content with human captivity. Good news of liberation of the oppressed from earthly bondage is what the Christian gospel is all about.

Professor Henlee H. Barnette, speaking to a Southern Baptist conference on Christianity and race relations at Glorieta, New Mexico, warned that some clergymen could corrupt the gospel to use it as a weapon to advance race hatred and prejudice. Dr. Barnette said that he had never known a racist who was an atheist.[142] Jesus founded the church and left it in the hands of men whom he empowered by the Holy Spirit to continue the work he began. Wherever there is need for justice, the church by its nature and mission should be there. King said that he was in Birmingham because injustice was there. He explained that just as the prophets of the 8th century B.C. left their villages and took their "thus saith the Lord" to other towns so he was compelled to carry the gospel of freedom far beyond the boundaries of his home town. King saw his ministry somewhat like Paul's also. For Paul, too, left his village of Tarsus and took the gospel of Jesus Christ to the far comers of the Greco-Roman world. Like Paul, he felt the need constantly to respond to the Macedonian call for help.[143]

King went everywhere he could in America to meet the need for justice. His protest marchers were basically members of the local church. He believed it was the moral responsibility of the church to move into those areas. All life was tied up in "a single garment of destiny," and no one could escape the network of mutuality. King believed that injustice anywhere was a threat to justice everywhere.

On August 28, 1963, Martin Luther King proclaimed in Washington, D.C., his dream of full integration of black and white America. He involved himself in protest after protest to make his dream come true. He believed man was a co-worker with God in the struggle for justice. His sudden and violent death left much work undone, many appointments unfulfilled. On the eve of his assassination he told a crowd in Memphis, Tennessee, that he was on the mountaintop and saw the promised land of integration. Blacks would get there, but he would not be included in the number.

For the blacks, King's dream is yet to be fulfilled, but they have seen so much accomplished by him in the cause of freedom that supporters and non supporters of nonviolence can wait and hope to see another rise up to lead them into realization of his dream. J. Claude Evans observes that it took the assassination of King to get the fair housing bill passed in the House of Representatives.[144] Evans interprets Kings violent death as the death of individualism as a method of solving humanity's social problems. Paradoxically, the death of King can assist the American dream toward fulfillment. For his violent death is a judgment on the individualistic attitude of all Americans. It forces each American to ask what he and his society have been doing for the sake of the American dream of democracy and the Judeo-Christian dream of the brotherhood of man. Out of this judgement can come the resurrection of a new social commitment for justice.

After the Korean War, returning black soldiers did not find acceptance in America. This same pattern continued during the Vietnam conflict. Black men were trained in the art of killing. They could kill effectively. They were militant and frustrated. They needed to vent their emotions of hatred and bitterness without directing them toward their oppressors, which would have resulted in nothing but regrettable destruction and further humiliation. The nonviolent protest marches led by King gave those blacks a legitimate expression of their feelings, and it served as a safety valve. It also nurtured a tolerance necessary to achieve their goals.[145]

King saved the American nation from the physical and moral catastrophe implied in Eldridge Cleaver's warning. He threatened that the blacks would get their manhood. He said they will get it, or the earth would be leveled by their attempts to gain it.[146] In all his struggles, King simply attempted to affirm basic human rights for the blacks which the United States Constitution guaranteed.

Martin Luther King agonized with his people who were crushed by the unjust laws of segregation. The white church did little to help the blacks, and the law was on the side of the establishment. The black pastor believed that the church's destiny was tied to Christian education. As a community leader, King assumed the responsibility to identify and to overcome the evils of ideological conflicts in racial discrimination.

Throughout his academic pilgrimage, King, whatever his special motivation, searched for a Christian model to fight racism in America. At Morehouse, his vocation was settled. King plunged into extensive research toward the answer to racial problems, and while at Crozer Theological Seminary, he discovered the key to the solution- "Satyagraha," which is truth-force or love-force-and nonresistant physical protest to the evils of segregation. At Boston University, King clarified his thinking and conceptualized his idea of the causes of racial conflicts. He arrived at a metaphysical and philosophical structure for his notion of a personal God and the dignity and worth of all human personality. Montgomery, Alabama, offered him the arena within which to continue the liberation drama and to appeal dynamically to the fact of emancipation which was proclaimed more than one hundred years ago by Abraham Lincoln.

Recalling the Montgomery Bus Boycott, King admitted he did not have the slightest idea he would have been caught up in a crisis which would involve nonviolent resistance. He went to Montgomery to be pastor at Dexter Avenue Baptist Church. He did not begin the protest or even suggest such. He simply responded to the people's call for a spokesman.[147] The Bus Boycott, for instance, was suggested by the Women's Political Council.[148] The march on Washington was born in the mind of A. Philip Randolph in January, 1941.[149] Randolph convinced King of the necessity of the march on the nation's capital in 1963.

Although repeatedly King said that he had no idea he would have been caught up in any way with a Civil Rights Movement, in looking back his childhood experiences and his education in the liberal arts and theology prepared him for the role as leader. His intense search for a regulating ideology which would overcome the conflicting forces of relativism and his clinging attachment to Ghandi's nonviolent method to obtain desired goals made it appear that even if he did not know he was definitely being groomed for the role. If mankind is tied and bound to relativism, then he has no hope of the vision or of' achieving the absolute good or standard. Whereas a balance of, say, evils regulates relativism, the submission to and through the power of love puts flesh on the absolute good and makes it visible and achievable on planet earth. This love must have a capacity to suffer, not only deserved suffering but also suffering beyond, which becomes undeserved suffering. It is in this realm where relativism is lifted to the good and the way of peace and to peace for mankind. It is like the experience of seeing and accepting a person as he is and always was for the first time. He may be someone you have known and worked with for a number of years. But for some known or unknown reason you were able to transcend the situation and looking down upon it you clearly recognize the "new" relationship which was always the "old" but clouded with the juxtaposition of relativism.

No, there is a truth and a right which is true and right, common to every man irrespective to race, creed or color. When Dr. King accepted the call to pastor the church in Montgomery, his mind was clear about these matters. It was just a matter of meeting the situation. When he found it, he could have said as Amos that the lion had roared and that he could do nothing else but to speak up for the cause of justice.

King, a privileged and prepared black preacher arrived on the historical scene when the Civil Rights Movement needed a spokesman. The congregation at Montgomery, Alabama, called him to pastor the Dexter Avenue Baptist Church, but the walls of Dexter could not limit his area of service. For, soon, in conjunction with his pastoral duties, he was also the leader of a Bus Boycott which triggered a gigantic movement of liberation for the black man in America. The role of the church is to be the liberative voice of the oppressed as well as the oppressor. Whereas the oppressed needs release from the manipulation of power, the oppressor needs liberation from his culture that makes him treat the poor as subhumans. There are moments, though not at the same time, when both the actor and the acted upon are most miserable. In those circumstances, the church could be the "voice of sanity" to the oppressor and an advocate for fairplay to the oppressed. Because of her function, the church must continuously transcend the status quo and be unhindered for dynamic reconciliative pronouncements, actions, and activities for brotherhood. In the church of Christ, people from all walks of life, whatever their concepts or ideological differences, should feel free, protected, and at peace in the fellowship around the Communion Table of the Lord. At that Holy Meal, all become one in Christ, partaking of the one body broken and drinking his blood which was shed for us.

King was a pastor at heart but prophetic in action. As a pastor, his concern continued to the end for those who were oppressed, as well as for those who were the oppressors. Even after he achieved national and international recognition in the struggle, King stayed with his church. Through his devotion to the church and his undeserved suffering in the nonviolent cause for social justice, King restored the faith of many in the church.[150] At the time of his death, King, the Civil Rights Leader, was assistant pastor to his father at Ebenezer Baptist Church, Atlanta, Georgia. In his prophetic role, the black Baptist pastor envisioned a world of true brotherhood with equal justice for all God's children. Often King quoted the words of the 8th century prophet Amos who called in Israel to let justice roll down as waters and righteousness as a mighty-rolling stream.[151] Like Amos, King saw that God demands a just and righteous society, and like Jesus, he laid down his life as an act of love for its realization.

ABOUT THE AUTHOR

Reverend Dr. Philip A. Rahming, J.P.

At the age of 14 years, Philip, the son of Arthur and Rebecca Rahming, was stricken with that deadly typhoid fever. Privately, the doctor attending him told his parents that he would not live, or if he did, he would be no good to himself or to society. But miraculously, however, Philip recovered to be a normal child.

Upon recovery, the youth returned to his books and studied up to the Senior Cambridge Level. He worked at the Telecommunications Government Department first as a telegraphist and later as an accountant. Meanwhile he kept on studying.

In September, 1961, Philip got enrolled at Calabar Theological College, Kingston, Jamaica. He graduated in May, 1965, he was ordained and installed as pastor of Kemp Road Mission Baptist Church in August of that same year. In 1967 Rahming was appointed chaplain to The Bahamas House of Assembly, now Parliament. He resigned in 1968 to attend Southern Baptist Theological Seminary in Louisville, Kentucky. There he received both his Master of Divinity Degree and the Post Graduate Master of Theology Degree. Later he read for his Doctor of Ministry Degree at United Theological Seminary in Dayton Ohio. The Rev. Dr. Rahming served as president of The Bahamas Christian Council, 1977 to 1980 and from 1983 to 1986. In 1979 it was his special privilege to welcome his holiness Pope John Paul II to The Bahamas in a very brief stopover in the region from Latin America to Rome.

At the time of CHOGM, (Commonwealth Heads of Government Meeting) in Nassau Bahamas, Her Majesty Queen Elizabeth II opened Elizabeth Estate in the Eastern Section of New Providence.

Dr. Rahming led the prayers. The Rev. Dr. Rahming wrote the Pledge of Allegiance to the Flag of The Commonwealth of The Bahamas, as well as the National Song: God Bless Our Sunny Clime. This song was the first runner up to the National Anthem written by the Rt. Hon. Timothy Gibson.

In 2019, the government of The Bahamas honored the author of the pledge with the title the Right Honorable. Presently he is pastor of Rehoboth Global Ministry. In 2018, he was honored by Her Majesty Queen Elizabeth II as an Officer of the British Empire, OBE.

BIBLIOGRAPHY

Primary Sources

Books

King, Martin Luther, Jr. *The Measure of a Man*. Philadelphia: The Christian Education Press, 1959.

—. *Strength to Love*. New York: Harper and Row. Publishers, 1964.

—. *Stride Toward Freedom*. New York: Harper and Brothers, Publishers, 1958.

—. *The Trumpet of Conscience*. London: Hodder and Stoughton Ltd., 1968.

—. *Where Do We Go From Here: Chaos or Community*. New York: Harper and Row, Publishers, 1967.

—. *Why We Can't Wait*. New York: The New American library, 1964.

—. *The Wisdom of Martin Luther King: In His Own Words,* ed. Bill Adler Books. New York: Lancer Books, 1968.

Periodicals

King, Martin Luther, Jr. "A View from the Mountaintop" (Dr. King's last message), Renewal, 9:3-4, April, 1969.

Unpublished Materials

King, Martin Luther, Jr. "The Church on the Frontier of Racial Tension." An Address at Southern Baptist Seminary Chapel, April, 1961. Tape available at James R Boyce Centennial Library, Louisville, Kentucky.

—. A dialogue with Southern Baptist students of the Christian Ethics Class on the nonviolent technique of the Civil Rights Movement, April 19, 1961. Tape available at James R Boyce Centennial Library, Louisville.

Secondary Sources

Books

Abraham, Henry J. *Freedom and the Court*. New York: Oxford University Press, 1967.

Barnette, Henlee H. *Introducing Christian Ethics*. Nashville: Broadman Press, 1961.

—. *The New Theology and Morality*. Philadelphia: The Westminster Press, 1967.

Bennett, Lerone, Jr. *What Manner of Man*. New York: Johnson Publishing Co., 1965.

Bleiweiss, Robert M. (ed.). *Marching to Freedom: The Life of Martin Luther King, Jr.* New York: The New American Library, 1969.

Carmichael, Stokely and C. V. Hamilton. *Black Power*. New York: Alfred A. Knopf, 1967.

Clayton, Ed. *Martin Luther King: The Peaceful Warrior*. New York: Washington Square Press, 1969.

Countryman, Vern (ed.) *Discrimination and the Law*. Chicago: The University of Chicago Press, 1965.

Cox, Alva I. *Christian Education in the Church Today*. Nashville: Graded Press, 1965.

Dodge, Ralph E. *The Pagan Church*. New York: F. B. Lippincott Co., 1968.

Frazier, E. Franklin. *The Negro Church in America*. New York: Schoken Books, 1963.

—. *The Negro In The United States*. New York: The Macmillan Co., 1967.

Haselden, Kyle. *Mandate for White Christians*. Richmond: John Knox Press, 1966.

Hill, Samuel S., Jr. *Southern Churches in Crises*. New York: Holt, Rinehart and Winston, 1966.

Ianniello, Lynne (ed.). *Milestones Along the March*. New York: Frederick A. Praeger, Publishers, 1965.

Johnston, George. *The Doctrine of the Church in the New Testament*. London: Cambridge University Press, 1943.

Johnston, Ruby Funchess. *The Development of Negro Religion*. New York: Philosophical Library, 1954.

Kennedy, Eugene C. *The People Are the Church*. New York: Doubleday and Co., 1969.

King, Coretta Scott, Jr. *My Life with Martin Luther King, Jr.* New York: Holt, Rinehart and Winston, 1969.

Lewis, David L. *KING: A Critical Biography*. New York: Praeger Publishers, 1970.

Lincoln, C. Eric (ed.) *Is Anybody Listening to Black America?* New York: The Seabury Press, 1968.

Lindgren, Alvin J. *Foundations for Purposeful Church Administration*. New York: Abingdon Press, 1965.

Long, Edward LeRoy, Jr. *A Survey of Christian Ethics*. New York: Oxford University Press, 1967.

McCall, Duke K. (e d.). *What is the Church?* Nashville: Broadman Press, 1958.

Macquarrie, John. *Three Issues in Ethics*. New York: Harper and Row, Publishers, 1970.

Miller, William Robert. *Martin Luther King, Jr.* New York: Avon Books, 1969.

Niebuhr, Reinhold. *The Nature and Destiny of Man*. New York: Charles Scribner's Sons, 1964.

Ramsey, Paul. *Christian Ethics and the Sit-in*. New York: Association Press, 1961.

Reddick, L. D. *Crusader Without Violence*. New York: Harper and Brothers, Publishers, 1959.

Schaller, Lyle E. *Community Organization: Conflict and Reconciliation*. Nashville: Abingdon Press, 1966.

Seifert, Harvey. *Power Where the Action is*. Philadelphia: The Westminster Press, 1946.

Sellers, James. *The South and Christian Ethics*. New York: Association Press, 1962.

---

1   *This anthem, first runner-up to the Bahamas National Anthem, was sung on October 14, 1985 in the presence of Her Majesty Queen Elizabeth II and some 25,000 persons. The Rev. Dr. Rahming is author of this musical piece.

ENDNOTES

1   Herbert Warren Richardson, "Martin Luther King— Unsung Theologian," *New Theology* No. 6. ed. Martin E. Marty and Dean G. Peerman (London: Macmillan Co., 1969), P. 178.

2   Ibid.

3   Robert M. Bleiweiss (ed.), *Marching to Freedom: The Life of Martin Luther King, Jr.* (New York: The American Library, Inc., 1969), p. 42.

4   Coretta Scott King, Jr., *My Life with Martin Luther King, Jr.* (New York: Holt, Rinehart and Winston, Ltd., 1969), p.78.

5   Bleiweiss, op. cit., p. 38.

6   Ibid., p. 42.

7   Ibid., p. 45.

8   Davis L. Lewis, *KING: A Critical Biography* (New York: Praeger Publishers Inc., 1970), p. 24.

9   Bleiweiss, op. cit., p. 52.

10   Martin Luther King, Jr., *Stride Toward Freedom* (New York: Harper and Brothers, Publishers. 1958), p. 91.

11   Ibid., p. 97.

12   Ibid., p. 97.

13   Ibid., p. 96.

14   Ibid., pp. 96-97.

15   Ibid., p. 100.

16   Ibid., p. 33.

17   Ibid., p. 42.

18   Coretta Scott King, Jr., op. cit., p. 112.

19   Ibid., p. 113.

20   Ibid., p. 119.

21   Martin Luther King, Jr., op. cit., p. 51.

22   Ibid.

23   Ibid., pp. 104-107.

24   Ibid.

25   Ibid., p. 62.

26   Ibid.

27   Ibid., p. 85.

28   Ibid., p. 112.

29   Ibid., pp. 116-117.

30   Ibid., p. 117.

31   Ibid., p. 120.

32   Ibid.

33   Ibid., p. 133.

34   Ibid., p. 141.

35   Ibid., p. 148.

36   Ibid., p. 153.

37   Ibid., p. 160.

38   Ibid., p. 161.

39   Ibid., p. 171.

40   Ibid., p. 23.

41   Martin Luther King, Jr., *Why We Can't Wait* (New York: The New American Library, Inc., 1964), p. 87.

42   Ibid.

43   Ibid., p. 123.

44   Ed Clayton, *Martin Luther King: The Peaceful Warrior.* (New York: Washington Square Press, 1969), p. 86.

45   William Robert Miller, *Martin Luther King, Jr.* (New York: Avon Books, 1969), p. 168.

46   Ibid., p. 242.

47   Martin Luther King, Jr., *Where Do We Go from Here: Chaos or Community* (New York: Harper and Row, Publishers Inc., 1967), p. 67.

48   Robert M. Bleiweiss (ed.) op. cit., p. 9.

49   Alan Richardson, *An Introduction to the Theology of the New Testament* (New York: Harper and Brothers, Publishers, 1959), p.256, as cited by Alvin J. Lindgren, *Foundation s for Purposeful Church Administration* (New York: Abingdon Press, 1965), pp. 48-52.

50   Martin Luther King, Jr., *Why We Can't Wait* (New York: The New American Library, Inc., 1964), p. 91.

51   Ibid., p. 90.

52   Ibid.

53   Ibid., p. 86.

54   Martin Luther King, Jr. *The Trumpet of Conscience* (London: Hodder and Stoughton Ltd., 1968), pp. 33-34.

55   Ibid., p. 37.

56   Martin Luther King, Jr., *The Wisdom of Martin Luther King: In His Own Words,* ed. Bill Adler Books, Inc. (New York: Lancer Books, 1968), p. 94.

57   Ibid.

58   Ibid., p. 116.

59   King, *Why We Can't Wait,* p. 92.

60   King, The Wisdom of Martin Luther King, pp. 125-126.

61   Ibid., p. 126.

62   Ibid.

63   William Robert Miller, *Martin Luther King, Jr.* (New York: Avon Books, 1969), p. 222.

64   Ibid., p. 235.

65   Ibid., p. 239.

66   Ibid., p. 252.

67   Ibid., p. 266.

68   King, *Wisdom of Martin Luther King*, p. 127.

69   Ibid., pp. 125-126.

70   Martin Luther King, Jr., *Stride Toward Freedom* (New York: Harper and Brothers, Publishers, 1958), pp. 85-86.

71   James H. Cone, "Black Consciousness and the Black Church," *Christianity and Crisis*, XXX, November 2 and 16, 1970, pp. 247-248.

72   King, *Why We Can't Wait*, p. 91.

73   Ibid.

74   Miller, *Martin Luther King, Jr.*, p. 237.

75   Ibid.

76   Herbert Warren Richardson, "Martin Luther King— Unsung Theologian," *New Theology No. 6*, ed. Martin E. Marty and Dean G. Peerman (London: Macmillan Co., 1969), p. 178.

77   Ibid., p. 180.

78   Ibid.

79   Ibid.

80   Martin Luther King, J r., *Strength to Love* (New York: Harper and Row, Publishers, Inc., 1964), p. 18.

81   Ibid.

82   Martin Luther King, Jr., "The Church on the Frontier of Racial Tension." An Address at Southern Baptist Seminary Chapel, April, 1961. Tape available at James P. Boyce Centennial Library, Louisville, Kentucky.

83   King, *The Wisdom of Martin Luther King*, p. 127.

84   William B. McClain, "The Genius of the Black Church," *Christianity and Crisis*, XXX, November 2 and 16, 1970, p. 250.

85   Reuben A. Sheares II, "Beyond White Theology," *Christianity and Crisis*, XXX, November 2 and 16, 1970, p. 229.

86   McClain, "The Genius of the Black Church," p. 250.

87   E. Franklin Frazier, *The Negro in the United States* (New York: The Macmillan Company, 1967), p. 74.

88   Ibid., p. 549.

89   Ibid.

90   Ibid., p 550.

91   Cone, "Black Consciousness," p. 249.

92   Ibid., p. 250.

93   Sheares II, "Beyond White Theology," p. 230.

94   Ibid.

95   Ibid., p. 231.

96   King, *Stride Toward Freedom*, p. 85.

97   Ibid.

98   Ibid.

99   Ibid., p. 86.

100 Ibid., pp. 86-87.

101 King, *Why We Can't Wait*, p. 87.

102 King, *The Wisdom of Martin Luther King*, p.124.

103 Ibid.

104 King, "The Church on the Frontier of Racial Tension," p. 3.

105 Ibid., p. 4.

106 Ibid., p. 5.

107 Ibid.

108 Ibid., pp. 5-6

109 Ibid., p. 6.

110 Ibid., p. 4.

111 Ibid.

112 Lerone Bennett, Jr., *What Manner of Man* (New York: Johnson Publishing Co., Inc., 1965), p. 141.

113 Ibid.

114 King, *The Trumpet of Conscience*, p. 33.

115 Ibid.

116 Ibid., p. 34.

117 Ibid., p. 92.

118 King, "The Church on the Frontier," p. 9.

119 Ibid.

120 King, *The Trumpet of Conscience*, p. 33.

121 Ibid.

122 Miller, *Martin Luther King, Jr.*, pp. 265-266.

123 King, *The Trumpet of Conscience*, p. 42.

124 Ibid., p. 81.

125 Ibid., pp. 81-82.

126 Ibid., p. 85.

127 Ibid., p. 86.

128 Ibid., p.82.

129 Ibid., p. 86.

130 Ibid., p. 92.

131 Miller, *Martin Luther King, Jr.*, p. 268.

132 Richardson, "Martin Luther King," p. 182.

133 Ibid.

134 Ibid., p. 184.

135 Ibid.

136 King, *Stride Toward Freedom*, p. 103.

137 Miller, *Martin Luther King, Jr.*, p. 299.

138 Joseph H. Fichter, "American Religion and the Negro," *Daedalus*, 94:1102, fn. 18, Fall, 1965.

139 Sheares II, "Beyond White Theology," p. 235.

140 McClain, "Genius of the Black Church," p. 251, citing Hegel.

141 Cone, "Black Consciousness," p. 245.

142 Kyle Haselden, *Mandate for White Christians* (Richmond: John Knox Press, 1966), p. 17

143 King, *Why We Can't Wait*, p. 77

144 J. Claude Evans, "Beyond Individualism and Collectivism," *The Christian Century*, Vol. 85:778- 779, June 12, 1968, p. 779.

145 King, *Why We Can't Wait*, p. 88.

146   Cone, "Black Consciousness," p. 250.

147   King, *Stride Toward Freedom*, p. 101.

148   Coretta Scott King, Jr., *My Life with Martin Luther King, Jr.* (New York: Holt, Rinehart and Winston, Ltd., 1969), p. 112.

149   Miller, *Martin Luther King, Jr.*, p. 22.

150   King, *Stride Toward Freedom*, p. 86.

151   King, *Why We Can't Wait*, p. 88.

Printed in the USA
CPSIA information can be obtained
at www.ICGtesting.com
CBHW040235231024
16239CB00062B/1002